Shandy on Sunday

Best Wishes

Christine Dodsworth

Shandy on Sunday

Christine Dodsworth

Matador
9 Priory Business Park,
Wistow Road, Kibworth Beauchamp,
Leicestershire. LE8 0RX
Tel: 0116 279 2299
Email: books@troubador.co.uk
Web: www.troubador.co.uk/matador
Twitter: @matadorbooks

ISBN 9781788038782

British Library Cataloguing in Publication Data.
A catalogue record for this book is available from the British Library.

Typeset in 11pt Minion Pro by Troubador Publishing Ltd, Leicester, UK

Matador is an imprint of Troubador Publishing Ltd

Printed and bound in Great Britain by TJ International Ltd, Padstow, Cornwall

For Julie, Sam, Cameron, Chloe, Bella, Luke and Josie

Ballad Of Nidderdale

By Richard M. Light

Oh Nidderdale, how I miss you,
Now seas between us lie;
And oft I see your smiling face,
Though not with human eye;
But Memory's vision brings to me
Those scenes I knew so well;
Oh! Nidderdale, how I miss you,
Far more than words can tell.

By your dear banks my lovely Nidd,
I oft was wont to stray.
Your gentle murmur charmed my ear,
And soothed my cares away;
And sometimes I would sit and fish,
Or in your waters swim;
Oh, lovely Nidd, of your dear charms
My memory grows not dim.

High up on Whernside's heathered slopes
I've seen your dale below;
And Gouthwaite's waters cradled there,
With sunlight all aglow;
Whilst from the crest of Guyscliffe's crags
I've oft seen York's fair plain;
Oh! Nidderdale, I pray one day
Your paths I'll walk again.

But if I never more return,
And in strange land end my days;
Until I draw my latest breath,
I'll ever sing your praise.
For though the years are rolling by,
As night must follow day,
I'll ne'er forget my Nidderdale.
You'll be my love for Aye.

Author's Note

This story is part memoir, part local history, part social history and part family history. I have done extensive research and drawn information from a variety of sources in writing this book, and if I have made mistakes then I sincerely apologise. Some names have been changed, but events, as I remember them, are true.

Acknowledgements

Two lovely ladies, Margaret Waite from Killinghall and Daphne Fallon from Bedford, for their generous help in my family history research.

Michael and David Light for allowing me to use their father's beautiful poem, 'Ballad of Nidderdale'; Jean MacQuarrie, Harrogate Advertiser, for allowing me to use family funeral announcements, obituaries and other excerpts from the Ackrill newspapers; Christine (née Pawson) and Ian Winchester; Angela and Robert Sansam of Dyke Bottom Cottage; Gloria Whittall; Malcolm Neesam, Harrogate historian; Geoff Deighton and Marion Brooks, Bilton Historical Society; Peter Eaton, Claro Community Archaeology; Katy Bradbury, PA, Harrogate Grammar School; Louise Foskett, Office for National Statistics; Judith Fox, map librarian, Reading University; Andrew Orgill MA Dip Lib, Senior Librarian, Royal Military Academy, Sandhurst; staff at Harrogate Reference Library; Nidderdale Museum, Pateley Bridge; Royal Hall, Pump Room and Turkish Baths, Harrogate; the Thalidomide Society; Susan Langridge, the Green Howards Museum; John and Brian Hodgson; Stephen Jenson; www.ancestry.co.uk; www.findmypast.co.uk; information from Wikipedia.

Thanks also to Philip Scott for (unwittingly) sowing the seed for this story.

Last but not least, thanks to my hubby Charles for suffering the growing pains of this book with me.

Contents

Me

I set my face on fire. It wasn't intentional and I wasn't playing with matches, not really. It was Geoffrey's fault, I suppose. He would be about twelve, and I was maybe four years old. He was at an age when he was surreptitiously experimenting with smoking. One day he got a box of Dad's matches and transferred some to a matchbox of his own, then hid it on a ledge in the back of the radio in the living room. I saw him do this.

On Saturday afternoon I retrieved the hidden matchbox. Dad was sitting facing the table and I was in an easy chair slightly behind him. Reaching in his side jacket pocket I lifted out his box of matches. It wasn't a secret movement, but he didn't feel my small hand in his side pocket. I was a good little girl and I wanted to replace the matches my brother had stolen. Of course it was an exceptionally stupid thing to do but I was very young and did not realise the danger.

Bent over the boxes, I transferred each match back in and the box began to fill. I pushed in one last match and the friction against the phosphorous tip ignited the whole box. Whoosh! Dad spun round and dealt with the situation calmly. My face was burnt, my eyebrows had gone and my fair hair was singed. He lathered my face with Tannafax Jelly (later called Tannaflavin) from the first aid kit, all the while talking calmly to me.

My mum was out shopping, and he met her at the front door when she came home. 'Christine has burnt herself but she's alright. Don't go and upset her – she hasn't cried,' he warned her.

So Mum rushed straight in and peered closely at my face. 'Whatever have you done? What a mess. You have ruined your face.'

I burst into tears.

'I told you not to go in and upset her,' Dad admonished.

When the doctor came, he said that Dad's prompt actions saved my face from being scarred for life. I don't know how long it took to heal, and I don't remember any pain. It must have been superficial as there is no lasting damage. I don't even remember if I had the words at the time to explain why I moved the matches, or if Geoffrey was reprimanded.

*

December 1945 and Dad is demobbed from serving in the Army during the Second World War. 1946 heralds the return of the banana to Britain after its absence during the war, and the bikini is invented. The population of Harrogate is approximately 49,300. Deaths recorded were: 291 males, 393 females, and 24 infants under one year old. There were 361 legitimate male births, 380 legitimate female births, 41 illegitimate male births and 44 illegitimate female births in Harrogate in that year.

And in between the 'Britain Can Make It' exhibition celebrating British design, and one of the coldest British winters of the twentieth century, a mewling and puking infant is born at 1 French Street, Harrogate. I was born at home and Mrs Baker, a neighbour, helped my mum. She became her life-long friend. The lying-in period after giving birth in those days was ten days, during which time the new mother was advised not to get out of bed at all. Mum told me later how everyone remarked on what beautiful skin I had. Maybe this was a ploy to let me know that I wasn't adopted. But then I am allowing that she had the forethought to say this. I don't know if anyone remarked on my mop of hair which shows in the photo I have of me as a baby with a roll of hair on the top of my head.

I was one of the Baby Boomers and my arrival was not greeted enthusiastically by my brother Geoffrey who was eight years old and a pre-war baby. On hearing me squawk he complained, 'I'd rather have an old hen. I suppose now we won't be able to go to the cinema any more in the evenings.'

He was right. My arrival curtailed the family's new-found freedom and their post-war jaunts.

Although the United States had a popular music chart, the Hit Parade did not officially start until 1952 in Britain, and figures were mostly based on sheet music sales. Big Bands were popular at the time, and also solo artists Frank Sinatra, Perry Como, Nat King Cole and Bing Crosby. Initially

Me as a baby. I don't think this hairstyle will catch on!

released in 1942 'White Christmas' by Bing Crosby was re-released by Decca Records and became a hit again at Christmas 1946. It became the biggest-selling single of all time.

It snowed heavily from January 1947 until March, and I nearly caught pneumonia. Steam filled the kitchen because Mum sat up one night with a boiling kettle as the water vapour helped me to breathe and eased my congested lungs so that I was not included with the 24 infants who died in Harrogate that year. There was deep snow and the coal from the pits froze solid in the wagons, and one by one the power stations shut down. Britain still ran on coal and within one week there were two million people unemployed and little food in the shops. Snow blocked roads and closed railway lines. The snow was followed by the inevitable floods, then by a scorching summer. But I have no memory of this as I was too young.

My earliest memory is of sitting in 'Dad's chair' by the fireside with my little legs just reaching the end of the seat cushion and my feet protruding over the edge...and accidentally wetting myself. After that the chair was relegated to Granny Hodgson's house where I am sure it suffered a similar fate far more often and to a greater degree.

I remember this photo being taken. I had an itch on my right leg, and the photographer was taking so long to take the picture, I just had to scratch my leg – and that's when he took the photo.

I was young when I was born and then grew older, so that's normal, unless you've seen the movie *The Curious Case of Benjamin Button* where his life was the other way round, being born looking old and wrinkled and becoming younger-looking as he grew older. I suppose I was normal too, with a normal upbringing, but normal is what you know. Everyone around me seemed to be doing the same things as our family. I certainly didn't think about things, just got on with them. I didn't always feel completely normal. I was skinny, and as I grew into puberty I had hairy arms, or so they seemed to me – little blonde hairs which weren't noticeable to anyone else, but I kept my cardigan on, even on hot days, so nobody would laugh at me.

When I was at Harrogate Grammar School, I was laughed at, but that was because of my liberty bodice. 'You've got to wear your liberty bodice or you'll catch your death of cold,' my mother remonstrated with me. She didn't have to get dressed with the other girls in the changing rooms after showers when we had our gym lessons. I suppose we girls were all self-conscious of our blossoming bodies when we were about twelve or thirteen years old, but I was the only one wearing a liberty bodice. If I had been devious I would have taken it off in the toilets beforehand, but I was guileless. So I was laughed at, until their interests switched to a fatty or four-eyes. But then again, I was a four-eyes too. Nobody noticed I couldn't see properly until I was ten years old and had an eye test at school. By that time I was a goody-two-shoes and always sat at the front of the class, while my friends always rushed to the back seats, trying to hide out of the way. My mum wouldn't pay for any attractive glasses so I had to wear the pink National Health Service glasses with the elasticated metal clips around my ears. When I was a teenager I hated them. My mother thought I was still a child. So I wore them in class and stumbled about the rest of the time.

But I survived, which was fairly common in those days. I was born on 21 October 1946, ten months after Dad's demob from the Army, and on Monday 5 July 1948 the National Health Service (NHS) came into being. Aneurin (Nye) Bevan, Labour's Minister of Health, was responsible for the formation of the NHS, where everyone, the poor included, could receive free medical treatment, dental treatment including dentures, wigs, artificial limbs, hearing aids, spectacles and free prescriptions. This was great if you were a bald, toothless, short-sighted, hard-of-hearing person with one leg.

Over five million spectacles were issued in the first year. There was a flood of people to surgeries, hospitals and chemists, and in the following years millions of people had received free dental treatment, hospital treatment and free spectacles, including my horrible pink ones.

So we were lucky; we had a health service 'from the cradle to the grave', paid for by National Insurance contributions, as it is today. So I had nice, kind Mr Bevan to thank for my spectacles. Not only did I get my sickly pink spectacles, but we had another treat at school: the school dentist. We had an initial dental check at school. If anyone needed a filling (which we all did as we had grown up with the sugar-laden syrupy orange juice, free on the NHS, which rotted our teeth) then we went to the school dental practice in town. It was great fun. The dentist rubbed his hands in glee, put a gas mask on a victim's face and administered 'laughing gas' as an anaesthetic. Whoever called it 'laughing gas'? I never laughed. Then he pulled out our teeth or drilled right through to our brains, put poisonous mercury filling in the hole and threw us out of the door staggering and confused. Then we had nightmares all night from the gas. If we entered the dentist's room in trepidation we were told that we were 'silly, there's nothing to it'.

Another good game was when the nit nurse came to school. Each pupil had to stand in front of the whole class, bow their head forward and have their hair parted and examined by the nit nurse, much as a monkey preens another monkey. But if she found any nits, the nurse didn't eat them. We were told 'only children with clean hair get nits'. Yeah, right. That made us feel good. I don't remember anyone having nits, though. Then she whipped us round to face her and examined our nails. If anyone was a nail-biter they had bitter aloes painted on their nails so it tasted vile if they put their hands in their mouths. I never bit my nails and could never understand why anyone would want to do so, but some did, and we could see them in class being torn between putting their fingers in their mouths to bite their nails and suffering the horrible taste, or not.

We had free school milk on the NHS. They were little tubby glass bottles containing a third of a pint of milk. Before morning break they were brought into the classroom in metal crates which sat on a desk in front of the window like a threat in front of our eyes. The sun streamed in and warmed the milk so it was luke-warm and sickly when we were forced to drink it. Oh yes, we were forced. It was free and we were very lucky to have it.

As a baby these pleasures were all in front of me and I was ignorantly unaware as I grew like a weed in the garden.

When I was two years old we moved from French Street to 14 Cheltenham Parade in Harrogate town centre where Dad worked for Morley's Painters and Decorators. We lived in the flat which was above the shop and Mr Morley's office.

Perhaps I should describe next something about Harrogate, the town where I was born, and the nearby area in Yorkshire, and introduce some of my ancestors and family members, and the events which happened in the 1950s and 1960s.

God's Own County

On the outskirts of Harrogate is Killinghall, where my farming Wardman family ancestors lived. There were family members in Hampsthwaite, Killinghall, Fewston, Braisty Woods and Hartwith near Brimham Rocks and other surrounding areas in Nidderdale close to Harrogate. Brimham Rocks is an area of millstone grit rock formations which have been weathered over millions of years into amazing and towering shapes over heather moorland. There are panoramic views over Nidderdale and sometimes York Minster can be seen in the distance. It is a great place for children to climb and run about. When one of my grandsons was small he said that Brimham Rocks was his favourite place in all the world, even though he had been on foreign holidays.

My grandad's sister, Florence Wardman, married Harry Beecroft in 1922 and they lived at Hill Top Farm, Fewston. I have a painting of the farm. Near Fewston Reservoir is Beecroft Plantation, presumably planted by an ancestor, and where a mountain biking track opened in 2013.

Pateley Bridge

The scenic area of Nidderdale is an Area of Outstanding Natural Beauty and the view of the Nidderdale valley before dropping down into Pateley Bridge from Harrogate is not to be missed. From the elevated position of the old churchyard of St. Mary's Church in the small town there are enviable far-reaching views of the dale.

In the churchyard there is a gravestone erected in the 1790s to the young children of a family. The thought-provoking words read:

All you that come our graves to see
As you are now, so once were we.
As we are now, so must you be.
We in our youths were snatched away
Therefore repent, make no delay.

Pateley Bridge is a lovely market town which boasts the oldest sweet shop in the world, trading since 1827, selling old-fashioned sweets in the authentic traditional shop in the High Street.

The amazing Nidderdale Museum is housed in the original Victorian workhouse in eleven separate rooms displaying a large collection of exhibits which depict the Yorkshire way of life. There are also some local documents which can be viewed for family history research, which I have seen. The old workhouse now has craft and design studios exhibiting ceramics, glass and stained glass, jewellery, millinery, stone carving and sculpture. Alister Colley, who was born in Harrogate, has his workshop Zeitgeist Fine Art there too, with his wife Claire as managing director. Alister paints his pictures as if through the eyes of a child. This best-selling artist was the official artist of the Grand Départ, Tour de France, when the stages were cycled in Yorkshire in 2014. We have two of his giclee ink paintings of Bettys Café, Harrogate.

If you want a typical Yorkshire 'grand day out' you should visit the Nidderdale Show, or 'Pateley Show' as it is known locally. It has been held here in September each year since 1895 and traditionally marks the end of the agricultural show season. It celebrates the finest of agricultural traditions with displays in many classes of livestock as well as produce and crafts, and is a wonderful place to visit. It is amusing to see a judge delve his hand into a hay exhibit to take a sniff as if he is smelling a perfume; or watch a prize-winning bull who has decided he doesn't want to parade round the ring, despite the efforts of several burly Yorkshire farmers. Yorkshire animals as well as Yorkshire men can be obstinate!

Another fantastic view of Nidderdale is from the Coldstones Cut on Greenhow Hill just outside Pateley Bridge. Coldstone Quarry is the last working limestone quarry of many which used to operate in the surrounding hills. It is also the highest at 1400 feet above sea level but, even though the quarry is huge, it is hidden from the road by its location and by a protective earth bund. The Coldstones Cut, constructed in 2010, is a monumental piece of public art, a sculpture which is an array of platforms from which visitors can see the quarrying operations, including blasting, extraction and crushing of rock to provide aggregate for building supplies for West and North Yorkshire.

Knaresborough

The ancient market town of Knaresborough on the River Nidd is situated about three miles east of Harrogate. It has a ruined Norman castle overlooking the gorge and is very picturesque with the railway viaduct over the river. Indeed, views of Knaresborough have adorned many a magazine cover and publication. Knaresborough's most famous resident was Mother Shipton who was reputedly born here in a cave in 1488. She was regarded as a witch and became well known as a fortune teller and is said to have foretold the Great Fire of London and the defeat of the Spanish Armada. The Petrifying Well (once called the Dropping Well) near Mother Shipton's Cave gradually turns objects to stone from the limestone in the water dripping over them, similar to the process which creates stalactites and stalagmites, but much faster. The well used to be regarded as magical, and it has always been a legendary place.

Although born in York in 1570, Guy Fawkes once lived in Scotton near Knaresborough, and there is now Guy Fawkes Arms in Scotton which serves delicious food.

Another famous inhabitant was Blind Jack of Knaresborough, John Metcalfe (1717-1810), who was a bridge builder and professional road builder during the Industrial Revolution. After losing his sight after smallpox infection at the age of six, he became an accomplished fiddler as a way to earn a living. He was a carrier (transporter of goods) and by 1754 his business had grown to a stagecoach line before an Act of Parliament in 1765 authorised the creation of toll roads and he won contracts to build roads.

On a sunny Sunday in the 1950s our family would catch the bus from Harrogate station to spend the afternoon in Knaresborough, enjoying an ice cream cornet and watching the boaters on the river who had hired rowing boats for the afternoon.

York

The historic walled county town of York lies further to the east of Harrogate, with its famous Minster dominating the skyline. It sits at the confluence of the rivers Ouse and Foss and was founded by the Romans. York grew as a major wool-trading centre. In the nineteenth century it became a hub of the railway network and now there is the great free-entry National Railway Museum in York displaying locomotives and exhibits with over 300 years of history.

York is also a confectionery manufacturing centre. Terry's of York was founded here in 1767 followed in 1862 by another chocolate manufacturer, Rowntree's Cocoa Works. At its peak more than 14,000 people were employed in the chocolate factories, and Rowntree's site at Haxby Road, which opened in 1890, was so big it had its own fire brigade. The workers could eat as many chocolates as they liked at work, but were never allowed to take them home. When the packers were filling the tins of chocolate to send to the troops in the First World War, they smuggled messages of support into the tins too.

The Shambles, York's oldest street, and Europe's best-preserved medieval street, is a row of overhanging timber-framed buildings where the roofs almost touch each other in the middle of the cobbled street. The buildings were originally used as butchers' shops, some dating as far back as the fourteenth century. You would have to be very wary if you walked down these old streets in bygone days as servants tipped the slops from the upstairs windows into the streets below after shouting a warning cry of 'gardyloo' derived from the French *gardez l'eau* – 'beware of the water'. This is possibly where the English word for toilet, 'loo', derives from. The people in the street would shelter under the overhanging eaves and there they could secretly listen to the conversations inside the houses, hence the word 'eavesdropping'. The butchers threw the guts, offal and blood into the channel in the middle of the street too. The drinking water became contaminated and that's why there was so much disease in the towns.

Ripley

Three miles to the north of Harrogate is Ripley with its Grade I listed castle which has been the home of the Ingilby family since 1320. Thomas

Ingilby (1310-1369) saved King Edward III from being gored by a wild boar while they were on a hunting expedition and was knighted for his deed. The Ingilby crest has a boar's head as a symbol. There are boar references around Ripley and there is the Boar's Head Hotel on the estate. In 1605 Sir William Ingilby (1546-1618), along with other family members and associates, was involved in the Gunpowder Plot. He allowed the plotters to stay at Ripley while they procured horses. The Gunpowder Plot was a failed attempt to blow up the Houses of Parliament during the State Opening. It was an assassination attempt on Protestant King James I of England and VI of Scotland by a group of English Catholics, the most well-known of which was Guy Fawkes. Celebrating the fact that the king had survived the attempt on his life, people around London lit bonfires, and months later the introduction of the *Observance of 5th November Act* enforced an annual public day of thanksgiving for the plot's failure. That's why we still celebrate Guy Fawkes Night on 5 November each year with firework displays and bonfires.

The largest battle ever fought on English soil took place on Marston Moor, not far from Harrogate, on 2 July 1644 during the English Civil War. After the battle, the victorious Parliamentarian general, Oliver Cromwell, billeted himself at Ripley Castle with some of his officers. The Royalist Lord Ingilby, who supported Charles I, had been routed in the battle and reputedly was hiding in a priest hole in the castle. Lady Ingilby was ordered to receive the victors and watched them vigilantly through the night until they left in the morning.

I remember walking from Bilton to the historic village of Ripley one Sunday with friends from Harrogate Grammar School, having one of the famous ice creams, sitting in the stocks, and then catching a bus back.

Ripon

Further north from Ripley is Ripon, given city status by its 1300-year-old cathedral. Charles Dodgson was canon of Ripon Cathedral from 1852 to 1868. He was the father of Charles Lutwidge Dodgson, better known as Lewis Carroll, author of the *Alice in Wonderland* stories. It is claimed that Ripon Cathedral was the inspiration for the stories. Under the choir stall seats are misericord carvings, one of which shows a griffin chasing a rabbit down a hole. On another misericord is a misshapen character with head and legs which looks rather like Alice when she shrank in size after eating a piece of mushroom. Also a James I Coat of Arms depicts a lion and a unicorn which appear in *Alice Through the Looking Glass.*

Wilfred Owen, the First World War poet, spent some time at the Northern Command Depot at Ripon on light regimental duties after he was discharged from hospital in Edinburgh where he had been treated for shell shock. While in Ripon he composed several poems, including 'Futility and Strange Meeting'. He spent his twenty-fifth birthday quietly at Ripon Cathedral. Despite being allowed to remain on home duty, Wilfred Owen saw it as his duty to write about the horrific realities of war, as Siegfried Sassoon had done. So in July 1918 Owen returned to active duty in France where, tragically, he was killed in action on 4 November 1918, one week before Armistice Day on 11 November.

Britain in the 1930s was suffering from the worldwide depression, and heavy industries were hardest hit. Palmer's shipyard in Jarrow, County Durham had been closed down in 1934 and there was 70% unemployment in the town. In October 1936, a group of 200 flat-capped men from the north-east town marched 300 miles to London to present a petition of 12,000 signatures to Parliament requesting the re-establishment of industry. The seventh stage of the march went through Ripon, Ripley, Killinghall and on to Harrogate before moving on to Leeds the next day. The Bishop of Ripon gave the marchers his blessing, and a subscription of £5. The petition was presented to Parliament but Stanley Baldwin, the Prime Minister, refused to see any of the marchers. Despite the support from the British public, there was little government support and the marchers felt they had failed. The outbreak of war in 1939 increased demand for coal and ships, and sufficient work returned to Jarrow and other affected areas. In subsequent years the Jarrow March became recognised as a defining event of the 1930s. It helped to foster the change in attitudes which led towards social reform.

In 1974 the singer Alan Price released the 'Jarrow Song', and in honour of the Jarrow Marchers, Lindisfarne, the folk rock group, released a song called 'Marshall Riley's Army' on their *Back and Forth* album in 1978. These songs helped raise awareness of the events of 1936 to a new generation.

Every evening at nine o'clock the Ripon Hornblower sounds the horn at the four corners of the obelisk in the market square to 'set the watch'. This has been a tradition since the year 886 when Alfred the Great visited Ripon and granted the city a Royal Charter and presented a horn as a symbol of the charter, as he did not have a parchment with him. The Wakeman was to stay awake at night and patrol the area to guard against Viking intruders. The Hornblower, dressed in a uniform and tri-cornered hat, still sounds the horn each evening as the custom has been for over 1000 years.

My father-in-law and mother-in-law were married in 1930 in the historic and majestic Ripon Cathedral, and both sets of their parents married in the cathedral too, his in 1904 and hers in 1906.

Fountains Abbey

Close to Ripon are the dramatic ruins of Fountains Abbey, a Cistercian monastery founded in 1132 and operated for over 400 years until 1539 when Henry VIII ordered the Dissolution of the Monasteries. It is one of the largest and best-preserved ruined Cistercian monasteries in England and is a Grade I listed building. Together with the surrounding water garden, deer park and Elizabethan manor house the area is a World Heritage Site.

Blubberhouses and Fewston

Blubberhouses is a small village in Fewston parish with a population of less than one hundred in the 2011 Census. The name is a corruption of blueberry or bilberry or possibly it may have derived its name from the 'blowers' or 'blauers' which was the local name for the iron-smelting factories. The population in Fewston parish in 1841 was 850 as there was an iron industry and mills. West House Mill, using water power from the river Washburn, was a five-storey flax mill and was one of the first in England to use the apprentice system for its workforce. When it was built it had one of the largest watermills in Europe. There had been a corn mill, then flax, linen and finally silk before the mill closed. It was a story of 'boom and bust' and the mill was eventually bought and demolished by Leeds Corporation Waterworks during the construction of reservoirs to provide pure water to Leeds seventeen miles away. Fewston Mill was pulled down in 1874 and West House Mill in 1877. The stone from West House Mill was used to build a wall around Fewston Reservoir. A former vicar of Fewston famously said, 'Fewston must die so that Leeds may live.' The grand mill-owner's house, West House Villas, was turned into Skaife Hall and was also owned by Leeds Corporation.

Blubberhouses Cricket Club was originally formed during the first half of the nineteenth century on land belonging to the Gill family of Blubberhouses Hall. Towards the end of the nineteenth century Colonel William Johnson Galloway, MP in Manchester, took Skaife Hall as his country residence and became President of the club, improved the ground, built a bandstand and held an annual cricket festival, which brought a degree of fame to the ground and to Blubberhouses, with national and international players taking part. These included George Ulyett who played for Yorkshire between 1873 and 1893, the Hon. F. S. Jackson who played for Yorkshire between 1890 and 1907, and B. J. T. Bosanquet, the player who invented the 'googly' which is when a cricket ball is bowled as if to break one way then actually breaks in the opposite direction.

After Colonel Galloway left Skaife Hall in 1924, Leeds Corporation did not let the house again and it gradually deteriorated until it was pulled down.

Bolton Abbey and Skipton

The Roman Road known as Watling Street runs in a straight diagonal line through the parish of Fewston. Part of it forms the A59 modern route between Harrogate and Skipton. West from Harrogate, over the wonderfully named Blubberhouse Moors on the A59, lie the picturesque ruins of Bolton Abbey on the River Wharfe. About six miles further on, lying on the River Aire and the 127-mile-long Leeds and Liverpool Canal, is the market town of Skipton, recorded in the Domesday Book of 1086. The canal is the longest in Britain and took more than forty years to build and has ninety-one locks. In its heyday it carried coal from Bradford's collieries and textiles from the mills to Liverpool. Skipton has a castle, first built in 1090 as a wooden structure, but later strengthened with a stone keep in the twelfth century. After the battle of Marston Moor it was the only stronghold in the north, and withstood a three-year siege. Eventually the Governor, Sir John Mallory, negotiated a surrender in December 1645. When the Parliamentarians took over the castle they commenced alterations, but work progressed slowly. General Lambert wrote to Cromwell 'The men come late, leave early, and stand idle while they are here.' Nothing changes then!

Otley

Another ancient market town, Otley, lies south west of Harrogate on the River Wharfe. It was in Otley that the cabinetmaker Thomas Chippendale was born in 1718 and his statue stands next to the old Grammar School where he attended.

J. M. W. Turner, the painter, visited Otley in 1797, aged twenty-two, when he was commissioned to paint watercolours of the area. He was so attracted to the area that he often returned and was a regular visitor at Farnley Hall where he was reputed to have been inspired to paint the stormy backdrop of 'Hannibal Crossing the Alps' by a storm over the Chevin (a gritstone escarpment). The foundation stones for the Houses of Parliament were hewn from a quarry on the Chevin.

Otley was also where I visited for a day in the 1960s and my boyfriend rowed us on the river. Unfortunately his right arm was stronger than his left and we kept going round in circles and running into the bank through the overhanging weeping willows and nearly went over the weir!

*

South of Harrogate are the large industrial towns of Leeds and Bradford where many people work, but choose to live in the greener, attractive town of Harrogate where there is no heavy industry.

In Yorkshire, not far from Harrogate, there are some strange place names such as Kettlesing Bottom, Summerbridge, Cowthorpe, Beckwithshaw, Bishop Monkton, Little Ribston, Follifoot, Burnt Yates, Smelthouses, Glasshouses, and of course Blubberhouses and Killinghall. And there is a Bedlam.

There are some unusual surnames in Yorkshire too, such as Pickersgill, Smurthwaite, Higginbottom, Heptinstall, Blenkinsop, Popplewell, Twisleton, Barraclough, Dollimore, Bendelow, Capstick and Crazy. Maybe there is a Crazy family in Bedlam!

The usual greeting in Yorkshire is 'Aye up!' or 'Ow do, love,' or a slight nod and 'Now then.'

If you ask, 'How are you?', often the reply is 'Mustn't grumble' or 'Ahm fair t' middlin'', or very rarely, 'Reet champion.' Yorkshire folk are 'the salt of the earth' and genuine. They 'call a spade a spade'.

The Pennines, rivers, valleys, hills, caves, limestone pavements and dry-stone walls of the Yorkshire Dales, and the heather moorland of the North York Moors lie roughly west and east of Harrogate. Most of the dales are named after their river or stream, as in Wharfedale, Airedale, Nidderdale, with the well-known exception of Wensleydale which is named after the small village of Wensley. There are many lovely towns and villages in Yorkshire. You should explore them for yourselves. Yorkshire is a glorious county and I wholeheartedly agree that it is 'God's Own County'.

Harrogate

If anyone asks, 'Where were you born?', and you reply 'Harrogate', they are impressed. People say what a lovely place it is or that they have always wanted to go there as they have heard it is so nice. It is. For the last three years it has also been voted the happiest place to live in the United Kingdom, up to 2016. So why did we leave? For advancement in my husband's career.

As I said, I was born in Harrogate, grew up there, went to primary school, and then the grammar school. I started work there in the Civil Service, got married in Harrogate and lived there until I was twenty-four years old and moved to Scotland with my husband in October 1971.

One of my ancestors, Myles Wardman de Haverah Park, was born in 1643 and died in 1714. I have a copy of his will made on 23 August 1714. The Forest of Knaresborough was a large tract of moorland with trees in its sheltered valleys, and within its borders were the two enclosed parks of Haverah and Bilton which were deer preserves. Haverah Park was once one of the royal parks attached to the Honour of Knaresborough and it lies on the western approach to Harrogate. Haverah is a corruption of Haywra, and according to the late Professor Skeat, Harrogate owes its name to the spot Haywra – gate. A gate is a way or path.

Harrogate developed from two small settlements: High Harrogate and Low Harrogate. It is a spa town, celebrated because of its mineral water springs which were discovered in the sixteenth century by William Slingsby. Hence, the town motto is '*Arx celebris fontibus*', which means 'a citadel famous for its springs'. These waters were said to have health benefits and among these curative waters are sulphur, chalybeate (iron) and magnesium minerals. There are more than eighty wells and no two of them are precisely alike. In the space of a quarter of an acre, more differing springs exist than in any other similar space in the world. Old Betty Lupton was an early celebrity who served out the Old Sulphur Water at the side of the spring in Low Harrogate for fifty-six years.

In the 1760s there was a widespread movement, nationally, towards enclosing Royal Forest land. If the land in Harrogate containing the wells and springs were to be sold, it would have been a serious threat to the community's prosperity. The hoteliers, innkeepers, shopkeepers and farmers would be deprived of their livelihoods. Representations were made to Parliament for an agreement for the land connecting the known mineral springs to remain open. In 1778 the Award of the Commissioners for the Enclosures of the Forest of Knaresborough established 200 acres of common in Harrogate to remain open and unenclosed for all people to have free perpetual access to the springs and to drink the waters. Rights to graze were also granted. This open ground, known as the Stray, surrounds the town and still remains unbuilt on and gives the town its unique style.

My *Ward Lock Illustrated Guide Book 1934-35* states that the Stray '*is a park-like common of 215 acres' and is 'open to everyone for riding or walking, and is a very popular resort among all classes – very different from the days just before the War when, according to a publication of the time, it presented "at all times a curiously Sunday appearance where none but the well-dressed are welcome."*

The name Stray is peculiar, and not met with elsewhere, and may arise from the agistment of cattle and sheep. Certain persons, owners of adjacent lands had the right to agist cattle etc. and in old maps, the Stray is called "The Stinted Pasture," which probably refers to its being pasture land rather than meadow. Those who had the protection of this common land were named "The Stray Gate Owners" and their functions were later vested in the Corporation.

A valuable provision is that the Stray may never be enclosed or built upon.'

It is a pleasant grassy area now, criss-crossed by paths, for people to walk their dogs, enjoy sport and glory in the spring crocuses at the border of the Stray and the pavement.

Hales Bar is the oldest pub in Harrogate with a history going back to the earliest days of the town's emergence as a leading spa resort. It was rebuilt in 1827 and known as the Promenade Inn, then enlarged in 1856 as Hodgson's, then William Hales became the landlord in 1882. There are still Victorian mirrors, gas lighting and cigar lighters in the lounge bar, and sulphur springs still flow beneath the cellar, notable by the distinctive odours which occasionally percolate up to the bar area, and the pub is reputed to be haunted!

In the 1800s wealthy visitors began to travel to Harrogate in carriages and coaches to bathe and 'take the waters' so that their ailments would be cured. Famous celebrities and foreign royalty came to stay in the town's hotels, principally the Granby Hotel, the Crown, the Dragon and the Queen's Head, and Harrogate prospered. A weekly list of visitors staying at the hotels in The Season (between May and September) was printed in the Harrogate newspapers. The Promenade Rooms opened on Swan Road in 1806 where visitors could socialise, showing off their fashionable clothes and listen to music. In 1839 the Promenade Rooms became the Victoria Reading Rooms and Library used for meetings and lectures. Then in 1875 it became a theatre hosting celebrities such as Lillie Langtry, Sarah Bernhardt and Oscar Wilde. Among other visitors to Harrogate in those times were Lord Byron, Charles Dickens, William Wordsworth and Robert Browning. Later the building became the Town Hall then council offices and now, since 1991, it is the beautiful Mercer Art Gallery.

In 1842 the octagonal Royal Pump Room was built over the Old Sulphur Well. It still is an iconic symbol of Harrogate. I should mention here that the sulphur water tastes and smells like rotten eggs. You only need one sip for its foul taste to repeat on you for hours afterwards, but in the heyday of the Pump Room people would arrive early in the morning from 7am to 9.30am and drink about two glasses before their breakfast. Visitors to the Pump Room were charged for drinking the water inside the building, but an outside tap was provided for anyone to drink the water free of charge at any time. This tap still exists and you could still drink the water until recently, but in 2012, despite an Act of Parliament which allows the water to be accessible by everyone, the European Union decided it was a health risk and the tap has been turned off! Surely, instead, there could have been a disclaimer as a warning for anyone drinking the water.

On Parliament Street is the jewellers Fattorini & Sons. The business was established by a family of Italian immigrants who arrived in Yorkshire in the early nineteenth century. Antonio Fattorini opened a shop in Harrogate in 1831 to take advantage of the seasonal trade. He also opened a shop in

The Pump Room in 1911.

Bradford in the 1850s. The firm began making sports trophies and medals, and also designed and made such famous trophies as the FA Cup and the Rugby League Challenge Cup which are both in use to this day. In 1967 we bought my diamond engagement ring from Fattorini's on Parliament Street!

John Farrah opened his now-famous shop in 1840. The Original Harrogate Toffee was designed to take away the putrid taste of the sulphur water, and the toffee is still produced in Harrogate. It is a hard toffee and is still made to the original recipe in copper pans, and the distinctive blue and silver tins are sold in shops including Selfridges and John Lewis and in various countries around the world. The product range now includes fudges, nougats, biscuits and preserves. At home we still use old Harrogate toffee tins for storing paperclips and pens.

On 20 July 1848 the railway came to Harrogate and the number of visitors to the town soared. The first railway station was Brunswick Station, diagonally across the road from the Brunswick Hotel (later the Prince of Wales Hotel and now the Prince of Wales Mansions) at the junction of Otley Road and Leeds Road. This station was in operation until 1 August 1862 when it closed to passengers and a new central railway station was opened which was more convenient for visitors to Harrogate for The Season, attending the balls, strolling in the gardens, listening to the early-morning band music and taking afternoon tea. The short tunnel which ran towards Brunswick Station is now bricked up but was reputed to have been used as an air raid shelter during the Second World War.

After taking the waters early in the morning, visitors returned to their hotels for breakfast, then retired for at least an hour to allow the waters to take effect and purge their bodies. Later in the morning they would possibly spend time in the shops on exclusive James Street, built in the 1860s with great arched windows divided by marble columns, or Parliament Street. By 1910 James Street had become the most fashionable street in Harrogate and James Ogden opened his prestigious jewellery business, with the beautiful Edwardian shopfront and showrooms, at number 38.

Harrogate has always been renowned for its shops, but the very wealthy visitors would not expect to go to the shops themselves, so the shops came to them. Mr Ogden would bring samples of jewellery from his respected business on James Street to the hotel where they would be displayed for the visitor. This led to the big hotels having display cases on the premises.

Next to Ogden's was another prestigious business, Marshall and Snellgrove, also built in 1910, which became the large department store of Hooper's.

The Victorian Lowther Arcade ran from Cambridge Street to Oxford Street and sold all manner of goods. The arcade had a mosaic tiled floor below an iron balcony.

A statue of Queen Victoria was erected in Station Square in 1887 to commemorate her Golden Jubilee. The statue shows her wearing ceremonial robes with a sash over her shoulder. It stands on a high plinth with a tall spire above to provide cover for it. Alderman Richard Ellis, who was Mayor at the time, donated the land and the statue with a clause to the effect that if Harrogate ever removed the statue, the land would revert to the Ellis family. Although there is a statue to Queen Victoria in Harrogate, as in many towns, she never actually visited Harrogate. The statue is still there, but the decorative ironwork and ornamental railings were removed during the national war effort in the Second World War and have never been restored. Many public buildings had their ornate ironworks removed to great beneficial effect during the war, but there was always too much iron to use and so a lot of it ended up in landfill or dumped at sea to avoid a public scandal.

The new Victoria Baths opened in 1871 followed by the Royal Baths in 1897 to offer spa treatments and hydrotherapy to visitors. All that is left of the working spa today is the Turkish Baths on Parliament Street. It is the best preserved, historically complete and fully working Victorian Baths in England. You can still have a Turkish baths experience and admire the brightly coloured glazed brick walls, Terrazzo mosaic floors, mahogany woodwork and reproduction Thomas Crapper toilet. The Winter Gardens next door was where people could relax amid potted palms and listen to music in the nineteenth century.

When the Jarrow Marchers reached Harrogate on 13 October 1936 hundreds of people lined the streets. Although a Tory town, Harrogate welcomed the Jarrow Crusade and a meeting was held at the Winter Gardens with Miss Ellen Wilkinson, Labour MP for Jarrow, as one of the speakers. The Winter Gardens is now a Wetherspoon's pub. It still retains some of its original architecture including its high ceilings, tiled floors and curved stone staircases.

Architect Frank Tugwell, who was also responsible for the Futuristic Theatre in Scarborough and the Savoy Theatre in London, designed the Grand Opera House which was opened in 1900 on Oxford Street and enjoyed full houses until the 1920s. Many of the day's top actors and actresses played there. The rise in popularity of radio and the cinema forced the Opera House to become a repertory theatre in 1933. The White Rose Players were one of the first permanent repertory companies in the country. Famous theatrical names included Sonia Dresdel, Trevor Howard, Brian Rix, Dulcie Gray, Rosamund John, Arthur Ridley and William Hartnell. Arthur Ridley played the elderly Private Godfrey in the *Dad's Army* TV programme from 1968 to 1977. William Hartnell who played the first Dr Who on TV from 1963 to 1966 apparently lodged with my Granny Hodgson while he was in Harrogate – and kicked her old black and white mongrel dog, Bobby.

Competition from television caused a decline in all live entertainments and Harrogate Theatre closed in 1955 but reopened again in 1958. With money from the Arts Council, the County Council and the Harrogate Corporation the theatre has been refurbished and is one of the most modern in the country and enjoys increased attendance. I lived with my mum, dad and brother Geoffrey on Cheltenham Parade from 1948 until 1956. We lived on the other side of the road from the stage door at the back of the theatre.

There are several churches and chapels in and around Harrogate. St. Mary's Church in Low Harrogate was built in 1825. This was where my Wardman great-grandparents, Thomas and Frances Anne Conyers, were married in 1881. Christ Church in High Harrogate was built in 1834. My Grandad Thomas Wardman and his sister Florence, who was a year younger, were baptised together there in 1886. Their older sister was baptised there in 1882. The Baptist Church on Victoria Avenue was where my Wardman grandparents, Thomas and Mary Ellen Moore, were married in 1906, and where I went to Brownies. My mum and dad were married in Wesley Chapel, Oxford Street in 1937. St. John's Church in Bilton was built in the 1850s. Its claim to fame is that I was supposed to be married there. I say 'supposed' because at the time six years of renovation and redesign work was planned and the heating system was to be replaced. So, when we went to see the vicar, the Reverend Vyvyan Watts-Jones, he rang the vicar of the nearby St. Luke's Church to see if we could be married there. His opening words on the phone were, 'Hello Hillary. This is Vyvyan,' to which we smiled at the apparently female names.

St. Peter's Church is in central Harrogate close to the Cenotaph. My dad said that there was a 'lazy' wind in Harrogate near St. Peter's Church – it blew through you instead of going round you! The climate in Harrogate is bracing, as the town occupies an elevated position and there is little to stop the easterly wind blowing from the North Sea, across the North York Moors, to St. Peter's Corner!

Sergeant Major Robert Johnston of the 8th Hussars, a Balaclava hero who died in 1882 age forty-nine, is buried in Grove Road Cemetery, Harrogate. He was one of the survivors of 'The Gallant Six Hundred' in 'The Charge of the Light Brigade' which took place on 25 October 1854. Poet Laureate Alfred Lord Tennyson wrote the poem 'The Charge of the Light Brigade' about the ill-fated cavalry charge into 'The Valley of Death' against Russian gunners deployed on three sides, during the Crimean War. There is an elaborate and imposing monument in Grove Road Cemetery, nearly eight feet high, erected to Sergeant Major Johnston, and sculpted by Thomas Potts.

The magnificent Hotel Majestic is a Victorian landmark in the centre of Harrogate, purpose-built in 1900 as a hotel and still a hotel today. The six-storey palatial red-brick building with its many windows, wide external staircase, portico and copper dome is certainly impressive. The opulent interior is traditionally decorated and has stunning Venetian chandeliers. It is set in eight acres of landscaped gardens with a sweeping promenade across the front of the hotel. A disastrous fire occurred in 1924 on the top floors of the hotel but the building was restored. On 12 September 1940 a German Junkers 88 plane dropped three bombs on the Majestic: one did not explode, another dropped in the grounds and shattered many windows, and the third demolished a nearby villa. These were the only bombs to drop on Harrogate during the war.

The Grand Hotel opened in 1903 overlooking the Valley Gardens, three years after the Hotel Majestic. The Grand certainly lived up to its name with five domes covered in gold leaf and a lounge hung with rich tapestries of old Harrogate. The Grand Hotel opened on 22 May 1903, six days before the opening of the Kursaal. My Aunt Cissie worked at the Grand Hotel.

Samson Fox, an English engineer, famous inventor and great benefactor, bought Grove House on Skipton Road in 1850. He installed a workshop in the basement where he invented water gas, and Grove House was the first house lit with water gas in the world. A suite of rooms was added for his friend the Prince of Wales (later King Edward VII) and his party when visiting Yorkshire. A self-made man, he had created the Leeds Forge Company, and invented the corrugated flue which made him a multi-millionaire. He was elected Mayor of Harrogate in 1890 and served for three successive years, a record not equalled since. A water gas plant was built to provide Parliament Street with the earliest street lighting in Europe. He was also instrumental in setting up the first fire service in Harrogate, and built Grove Road School.

The Kursaal, designed by Robert Beale and Frank Matcham, and funded by local benefactors led by Samson Fox, was opened in 1903 for grand receptions and special occasions to complement Harrogate's development as a spa. Samson Fox campaigned for the Kursaal to be as magnificent as possible. Sarah Bernhardt, Lillie Langtry and Harry Lauder were among the entertainers in the early years. At the outbreak of the First World War the Germanic name was changed to the Royal Hall although the original name can still be seen in the stonework. Samson Fox is an ancestor of the Fox family acting dynasty. He is the great-grandfather of distinguished actors Edward Fox OBE, James Fox OBE, and film and theatre producer Robert Fox, and great-great-grandfather to actors Emilia Fox, Lydia Fox, Freddie Fox, Laurence Fox and Jack Fox.

Harrogate has one of the original Carnegie Libraries, opened in 1906 on Victoria Avenue, with a donation of £7,500 from the philanthropist Andrew Carnegie towards the cost of more than £10,000.

Andrew Carnegie was born in Dunfermline, Scotland in 1835. He emigrated to the United States with his parents when he was thirteen years old and by 1850 he was working as a telegrapher. By the 1860s he had investments in railroads, sleeping cars, bridges and oil derricks. He became one of the richest Americans ever, but gave away almost 90% of his wealth in his later years, mostly to local libraries, education and scientific research. His name is prominently displayed in the brickwork at Harrogate library and there is a plaque near the door describing the background and the opening of the library. In 1930 the art gallery was added on the first floor. The library gardens are alongside the library (obviously!) and that is where my Grandma Wardman would take her leftover bread to feed the birds. Although the library was near my school, St. Peter's Primary School, I rarely went into the library as my parents were not great readers and, sadly, I did not read a great deal in those days. After being closed for nearly two years during a major refurbishment and extension, the library was reopened in October 2010.

At the top of the slope of Parliament Street is the renowned Bettys Café Tea Rooms where my mum worked serving cakes, biscuits and bread in the shop. Bettys was originally written with an apostrophe before the s, but at some point the apostrophe was dropped. Taylors of Harrogate merged with Bettys in 1962 and Taylors coffees and teas are consumed in the elegant café, served by waitresses in black and white uniforms and accompanied by a pianist. The original Betty's was opened in July 1919 by Frederick Belmont, a Swiss confectioner, across the road on Cambridge Crescent. I remember this shop and looking longingly through the window every Easter at the huge decorated chocolate egg.

My wedding reception was held in the Imperial Room on the first floor of Bettys overlooking Parliament Street on one side and Montpellier Gardens on the other.

In the centre of town, surrounded by flowerbeds, stands the huge Harrogate Cenotaph or war memorial, which was erected in 1922 to commemorate the Harrogate people who died in World War I 1914-1918. My Great Uncle Francis Henry Wardman, who was killed in 1917 and is buried in St. Seven Cemetery, Rouen, is commemorated there and listed as H. Wardman. Names of those who died in World War II 1939-1945 were added later to the Cenotaph.

Just off Parliament Street is Parliament Terrace, a row of Georgian, stone terrace houses opposite the Herald Buildings which was the home of Ackrill Newspapers which printed the *Harrogate Herald* and *Harrogate Advertiser* where John Craven, the journalist and TV presenter, started his professional career. Each of the houses had a stone-built outside toilet, no bathroom. These toilets have now been demolished or turned into storage buildings. The small back yards were all connected to allow the people at the bottom egress to the top near Parliament Street. At the bottom of the yards was a stone wall. The front of the terrace ran down to an alleyway which nowadays opens onto a mews, called the Montpellier Quarter, where there are antique shops, jewellery shops, cafés and restaurants. It is a very trendy area and, being slap bang in the centre of Harrogate, Parliament Terrace is a sought-after area for redevelopment by property developers. On a visit to Harrogate in 2008, 7 Parliament Terrace was for sale at £250,000. This is the house my Granny Hodgson lived in for over forty years.

Grandad Hodgson and the Army in India

Henry's parents, William Hodgson and Mary (nee Carpenter), had twelve children. Henry, born on 12 February 1876, was the eldest. The second child was Thomas who died on 2 February 1880 aged twenty-three months, six days after being accidently scalded by a pail of boiling water on washday.

Henry's brother Fred was killed in France during the First World War. He is mentioned on the gravestone where his father William and his mother Mary are buried in Middleton Cemetery.

The Commonwealth War Graves Commission states:

In Memory of
Private FRED HODGSON

3277, 5TH Bn., Yorkshire Regiment
Who died aged 23
On 24th December 1915
Son of William Hodgson, of Manor House, Middleton, Pickering
Yorks.
Remembered with honour
YPRES (MENIN GATE) MEMORIAL

He was actually killed on Christmas Day. There was supposed to be a Christmas Day truce, a cease-fire for the day. Fred put his head above the parapet of his trench and was shot by a German sniper and killed.

*

William was a tenant farmer at the Fox and Rabbit Inn and adjacent land. Then he took the tenancy of Mount Pleasant and Warren Farms, Lockton. After the death of his wife Mary on Christmas Day 1907, William purchased Manor Farm, Middleton, Pickering, farming there with his sons Robert and Walter until his death in 1927 when he was seventy-four years old. William was an illiterate farmer but he built up a prosperous farm and provided well for his family. When Henry was young, he was not interested in farming, so he joined the Army. He was a regular soldier in the Army for twenty-two years, first in the 12th Royal Lancers, then the Green Howards and finally in the Indian Army, and was invalided out as a warrant officer (the highest rank of Non-Commissioned Officer) with a pension of £110 a year in 1915 after his third bout of malaria.

Henry then met Emily in Harrogate and they lived in Parliament Terrace in the centre of Harrogate. Their three children followed in quick succession: my mum Vera born in 1918, Uncle Fred in 1919 (he was named after his Uncle Fred who was killed on Christmas Day in the First World War) and Clarence William (Uncle Bill) in 1920. Bill was always known by his shortened middle name of Bill because he hated the name Clarence.

After retiring from the Army, it seems Henry was not able to find meaningful work, but he earned £1 a week cleaning Barclays Bank, plus his army pension of £2 3s 4d. He enjoyed gardening and had an allotment at the top of Cornwall Road. As he had been in the Army, I think he was a strict disciplinarian as a parent, and my mum had a harsh upbringing.

Henry's malaria kept recurring and he died of pneumonia in 1936 when he was sixty and when my mum, Vera, was seventeen years old.

From the *Harrogate Advertiser, Saturday 7 March 1936:*

LURE OF THE COLOURS

Funeral of Travelled Ex-Soldier
The late Mr Henry Hodgson

The funeral of Mr Henry Hodgson, a retired Army Warrant Officer, of 7, Parliament Terrace, Harrogate, who passed away suddenly on Thursday, aged 60, took place at Stonefall Cemetery on Monday.

Mr Hodgson joined the Army in 1893, and served in the 12th Royal Lancers, stationed in Edinburgh. He then purchased his discharge and returned to civilian occupation, but the lure of the colours proved too strong, and he enlisted with the Green Howards at Richmond, Yorkshire. He served with this famous regiment in Jersey and Ireland, and was then drafted to India on his twentieth birthday.

Mr Hodgson took part in the Tirah Campaign of 1897-98, for which he received the Tirah medal with two clasps, and while on service in the Khyber Pass was promoted to the rank of lance-corporal. The battalion subsequently returned to Peshawar, and later went to Dagshal, where he was appointed cantonment overseer, and engaged in sanitary inspection with the local rank of sergeant. He was afterwards employed as staff clerk at Sitapur and Cawnpore, and was then promoted to corporal and then lance-sergeant.

Served at Calcutta

In 1904 he left the Green Howards and was transferred to the Indian Army unattached list with the rank of staff sergeant. He became a barrack master and served at Calcutta and Dinapur. In 1913 he was gazetted warrant officer, and retired at the end of 1915 owing to ill-health. Six months afterwards he was registered lieut-quartermaster of the new service battalions.

During the early part of the Great War Mr Hodgson was engaged at Quetta in despatching stores to Mesopotamia. During his Army service he acquired proficiency in three languages – Hindustani, Pushtu and Burmese.

In 1925 considerable local interest was aroused by a series of letters he received from General Sir William Birdwood, then Commander-in-Chief in India, with whom he served in the 12th Lancers.

Mr Hodgson did not take much part in public life, although he was associated with the Harrogate Horticultural Association.

The Interment

The Rev. J. H. Bodgener (Wesley Church) officiated at the funeral service.

My Grandad Henry Hodgson. This was probably taken about the early 1900s.

There is not much information about Henry's Army service at the Green Howards Museum in Richmond, Yorkshire, or the Indian Army Records at the British Library in London, or the National Archives at Kew. His service record appears to have been one of those destroyed during the Second World War.

More than nine million men and women are estimated to have served in the British armed forces during the First World War. By the end of the war in 1918, more than seven million men and women had served in the British Army. Many of the surviving army records from this period can be found in the National Archives at Kew. Unfortunately, more than half of these records were destroyed in September 1940, when a German bombing raid struck the War Office repository in Arnside Street, London where the First World War records were kept. However, an estimated 2.8 million service records survived the bombing or were reconstructed from the records of the Ministry of Pensions. This means that there is roughly a 40% chance of finding a service record of a soldier who was discharged at some time between 1914 and 1920. But I can't find Henry Hodgson's.

The Green Howards Gazette (then called Ours) dated October 1894 lists 4550 H. Hodgson when he was assigned to F Company on enlistment and completion of training. He first served with the 1st Battalion in Jersey, then was transferred to the 2nd Battalion to embark for India. From his obituary in the Harrogate newspaper, that would have been on 12 February 1896.

In June 1897, across Britain and its Empire, celebrations were taking part for Queen Victoria's Diamond Jubilee. In Ranikhet in India, the 2nd Battalion celebrated with a week of festivities, including a ball and a gymkhana. Huge bonfires on the surrounding hills formed part of a vast chain along India's northern border. Unfortunately, this celebration of imperial pride coincided with the most formidable uprising ever of the Pathan tribesmen of the North-Western Frontier. Stirred to religious fervour by their Mullahs (religious teachers), the border between India and Afghanistan was quickly ablaze. The security of the entire frontier was in jeopardy.

The most powerful and numerous tribe were the Afridi who, with the Orakzai, occupied the area known as the Tirah, to the west of Peshawar. Its rugged mountains were bisected by fertile and prosperous valleys. Little of this unmapped Tirah had previously even been seen by any European. The boast of its warlike inhabitants was that no Mogul, Afghan, Persian or British army had ever penetrated their country.

The 2nd Green Howards, commanded by Lieutenant-Colonel W. E. Franklin, joined a 17,000-strong force at Kohat, poised to penetrate the Tirah. Before the 1920s the Green Howards were known as the Prince of Wales' Own (Yorkshire Regiment). The Tirah Expeditionary Force consisted of about a third British troops and the rest Indian Sikhs and Gurkha Rifles. Because religion and caste forbade Indian troops from menial tasks, a long tail of civilian 'followers' always accompanied any force. On 18 October the Green Howards took the dusty road out of Kohat. The snake-like columns of fighting troops, guns, transport and followers in the single mountainous track were protected by picquets (small units of military men) in the hills above, as they made their slow progress forward. The speed and aggression with which the enemy tribesmen followed the withdrawing picquets was dismaying. The foe was often well armed with captured or stolen rifles, and their shooting was effective. They were attacked on all sides by a force they seldom saw. No wounded could ever be left behind to face a horrible death by mutilation, often at the hands of the women.

They bivouacked, and spent a very cold and uncomfortable night, as the ration mules had not arrived and they had nothing to eat. The men were dressed in thin khaki, because their issue of thick khaki-coloured pea jackets, Cardigan waistcoats, Balaclava caps and warm mitts were on the mules too. The temperatures could vary a hundred degrees Fahrenheit between dawn and midday.

They eventually pushed the enemy back and penetrated into the Tirah interior and burnt and razed houses, the only method by which the enemy could be driven to submit. Other armies might have slaughtered any inhabitants they could catch, but the British Army did not practise what is now known as genocide.

The Afridis waged continual guerrilla warfare, and troops engaged in foraging or survey duties were constantly attacked. In December the Expeditionary Force prepared to evacuate the Tirah. The cold was intense, with twenty degrees of frost being registered. The 1st Division returned via the Mastura Valley and, though arduous, met little resistance. The 2nd Division marched by a different route, along the Bara Valley (thirty-four miles) and had to fight desperately for five days, bearing its wounded on dhoolies (stretchers slung on poles carried by four men). The path crossed and recrossed the icy stream, while snow, sleet and rain fell constantly.

The Battalion met up and pitched camp on 19 December near the famous Khyber Pass. The Khyber Pass and its forts were taken. The Afridi had had enough. Clan after clan submitted after realising further resistance was futile.

Negotiations for peace were then begun with the Afridis who, under the threat of another expedition into the Tirah in the spring, agreed to pay the fines and surrender the rifles demanded. The Expeditionary Force was broken up on 4 April 1898.

General Sir William Lockhart issued the following farewell to the force:

Tirah Expeditionary Force orders by General Sir W. S. A. Lockhart K.C.B.,
K.C.S.I., commanding.
Camp Peshawar,
4th April, 1898.

On relinquishing the command of the Tirah Expeditionary Force, which is about to be reduced to a single division, I thank all ranks for the work which through their bravery and devotion has been successfully accomplished in the past six months.

From the beginning of October to the middle of January the Force was engaged in active operations, and seldom have troops been called upon to undergo greater fatigue, or to meet a more vigilant and enterprising enemy. After long marches in cold and wet, harassed by distant rifle fire and by assaults at close quarters, the columns bivouacked in positions which had to be protected by numerous strong picquets posted on commanding heights, and those picquets were always liable to determined attacks, and to molestation on withdrawal. There was, in fact, little or no rest for the force, the most carefully chosen camping ground being generally open to long-range fire from scattered individual marksmen armed with the most accurate weapons.

I congratulate the soldiers under my command on the successful result of the operations. In no previous campaign on the North-West Frontier have the difficulties to be overcome been more formidable; in none has the punishment been more exemplary, or their submission more complete.

W. S. Lockhart, General
Commanding Tirah Expeditionary Force.

On the demobilisation of the Force the following complimentary order was issued by Major-General Sir W. Penn Symonds, K.C.B., under whose command the battalion had served for over eight months:

I have nothing but praise to give the 2nd Battalion Yorkshire Regiment for their good work and good service during the Tirah Campaign, and whilst under my command I have formed a high opinion of the battalion, and have had the greatest pleasure in always reporting very favourably on it. Your patience and cheerfulness – both valuable soldierly qualities – lately displayed under very trying circumstances have earned my warm approval. I wish you all good fortune.

The 2nd Battalion was to serve in India for eight more years.

Granny Hodgson

Granny Hodgson was a stooped, diminutive old lady bent like a boomerang by undiagnosed osteoporosis. She smelt of Wintergreen Ointment which she used to ease her aches and pains. The unctuous smell emanated from her layers of clothing and thick Lisle stockings, and hung around her frail frame like an aura. She had a disconcerting habit of shuffling to her back door, opening it wide and hollering, 'Mama's baby', to anyone who might be within earshot. This happened as she was looking after me when I was a small child, and my mum was at work. I don't know if anyone else was aware of her strange habit. I certainly wasn't going to tell them. She was bonkers. I am sure my family think I am a daft old bat, but I am a gran now and that's my prerogative.

Of course Granny wasn't always old, but that's how I remember her. Geoffrey, who was a pre-Second World War baby, and therefore eight years older than me, would think of her as not-quite-so-old.

Granny Hodgson wore the full spectrum of colours, as long as they were grey or brown, like the interior of her house. The house was rented and she had lived there for over forty years when she died, so she had paid rent all that time and did not own a brick (or stone). In the early years she lived in the small terrace house with Henry and their three children. I can't say he was Granny's husband, because he wasn't.

'I have been doing some family history research, but I can't trace your mum and dad's marriage certificate,' I said to Uncle Bill on a visit to see him and Auntie Freda at their home in Deal in Kent some years ago.

'Oh no, you won't find it. They were never married,' he informed me.

Shocked, Freda turned to him and exclaimed, 'I never knew that. All the forty years we have been married and you never mentioned that to me!'

Granny Hodgson in the early 1960s when she was about eighty years old.

Well, well. So Granny Hodgson, who was referred to on all legal documents as Emily Hodgson, was still, in fact, Emily Knowles.

'Well, he was already married. He was married near Pickering, Yorkshire where he was born. He was in the Army and apparently she was unhappy to be an army wife and didn't want to go to India. Some years later he met my mum in Harrogate and they lived together as man and wife for the rest of his life. Emily's parents may have died young as she was brought up by an aunt,' Uncle Bill told me.

I researched and traced Henry's marriage certificate. On 16 January 1902, when he was twenty-five years old, he married Sarah Thompson at the parish church in Middleton. She was twenty-seven and their address is given as Lockton. Henry was a lance corporal and his father William is stated as a farmer. John Thompson, Sarah's father, is stated as an inn keeper. Divorce was very difficult and extremely expensive in those days. When Henry was invalided out of the Army in 1915 he must have met Emily in Harrogate and they set up home together.

When Henry's father William died in 1927 he left his farm of 122 acres to his sons Robert and Walter. He also bequeathed a total of £5,000 (about

£280,000 in today's terms in 2017) immediately to his sons and daughters in Pickering. His will states, *I William Hodgson of Middleton near Pickering in the County of York, Yeoman... bequeath the sum of two hundred pounds to my son Henry in ten yearly instalments of twenty pounds each* (about £1,120 a year today), *and if the said Henry should die in my lifetime or in the duration of ten years from my death, the instalments of such sum of two hundred pounds or the balance remaining shall be applied to the maintenance of his illegitimate children Vera, Fred and William.* (Got his favourite name right! Of course he was his namesake after all.)

The will goes on further to say that *out of the rents and profits of my farm the annual sum of one hundred and twenty pounds to my four daughters Mary Ann Hodgson, Annie Hodgson, Jane Elizabeth Hodgson and Minnie Johnson... and after the death of the last survivor to sell my farm and divide the net proceeds between all my grandchildren.* He actually mentioned the names of Henry's children in the will. The terms of the will were not all adhered to as the farm was sold long before the daughters died. I believe Henry's family never received anything from the sale, as the executors were John William Hodgson and George Hodgson, Henry's brothers. They presumably kept the money within the rest of the family in the Pickering area. Who ensures that the executors of a will carry out the instructions?

So when Henry died in 1936, Emily was left with her three children and not much else. In later years, when I was a child, she rented out the ground floor front room to lodgers when she could. This room was off the hallway, near the front door, and was sometimes rented to touring actors from the nearby Harrogate Theatre.

*

The house still looks the same from the outside, a mid-row Yorkshire stone terrace house just off the splendid Parliament Street in Harrogate. I didn't tell the estate agent that my granny had lived there, that I was on a journey back in time to revisit my past. He thought I was a potential buyer ready to pay £250,000 for the property in the now-trendy mews area. I saw that some of the old outside toilets had been demolished or were being used as sheds. The back yards which had been sloping were levelled and turned into small patios with tables and chairs.

I shouldn't have gone inside. The house had been totally refurbished, understandably so, but still I was surprised. The memories remain vivid in my mind, but in reality now, all traces of Granny Hodgson and her way of life have been obliterated. The house was Granny and Granny was the house. She hardly ever left it in my young years, and certainly less often after her accident.

The wall which separated the hallway from the front room has gone to enlarge the room, which is now a dining room with a hole-in-the-wall fire. The kitchen has a laminate floor and built-in Farrow and Ball units, all cream and sparkling. Upstairs Granny's bedroom has gone altogether and surprises me as a fully-tiled wet room with a large shower and bath. Across the top of the stairs Uncle Fred's bedroom has become the lounge with an imposing plasma screen TV on the wall.

I remember a narrow hallway, decorated in lincrusta (an embossed wallpaper similar to anaglypta) and painted dark brown, with a large photo of Sir William Birdwood hanging proudly on the wall. The front room was never used, as I remember, only rented out occasionally. It had a dusty three-piece suite, chest of drawers and a fireplace.

The hall led from the front door to the kitchen at the back. It wasn't just a kitchen but a dining room and living room. All the daytime activities went on in this one room. There was a big black Yorkist Range fire with an in-built oven next to the fire. A brass companion set comprising tongs (for the coal), shovel and brush gleamed on the hearth. On a morning Granny would spread old newspaper out on the table and clean the grate with black lead polish while eating her boiled egg and toast. Her fingers busied between her pieces of toast and the black polish. With blackened hands she dunked her 'soldier' into the egg, popped it into her mouth, then continued with the blackening. Dribbles of egg yolk escaped from the sides of her mouth and trickled down her chin. She did not have her false teeth in at that time in the morning and her lips went up to her nose and down to her chin when she chewed. I was mesmerised. It was unnerving. Most old people had false teeth. Whenever teeth went bad, the dentist filled them with mercury filling or whipped the offending tooth out altogether after an anaesthetic of gas administered through a facemask. At night Granny cleaned her false teeth and then put them in a beaker of water overnight at her bedside, a disconcerting sight. They looked ready to snap anyone's careless finger off.

Granny could twist her long fine white hair into a perfect bun at the back of her head and anchor it with hairpins, with the expertise of many years. When she became ill and had to go into hospital towards the end of her years, her long hair was cut short and clipped at the sides with hair clips. I don't know how she felt about this, but maybe she was not too aware. Her memory was going. Maybe she had Alzheimer's disease which did not seem to be known at the time, or was not diagnosed.

The kitchen also had a Belfast sink with a wooden draining board positioned under the window so there was a perfect view of the concrete back yard and stone toilet when you were doing the washing up. The toilet was a cold, horrible place where I rushed in, spent as little time as possible, and then dashed out again. It was bleak. There was a nail on the back of the wooden door to which pieces of torn newspaper were impaled. This was our toilet paper, which was eventually superseded by the white, shiny, slippy Izal toilet rolls which were just as useless, but you couldn't read them as you could the newspaper.

Next to the sink was the modern oven which had overtaken the cooking in the Yorkist Range. Granny could make the best little Yorkshire puddings, crispy on the outside, and covered in brown Oxo gravy. She served them the Yorkshire way: Yorkshire puddings first to fill you up before the meat course. Uncle Fred would come home for lunch and get the lion's share of puds. My allocation was one, but I could always have eaten more.

A sideboard stood against the back wall. It contained a tablecloth, and crockery and cutlery. Sometimes we would spread newspaper on the table and polish the silver cutlery together. In the bottom of the sideboard was an old gas mask, a relic from the war. Presumably, as Granny had lived through two world wars, she kept the mask in case it was ever needed again.

On top of the sideboard stood a huge wooden radio the size of a large suitcase, with a rounded top, and mesh radiated out from where the sound emitted. Next to that stood a wind-up gramophone which I loved to play, and which Granny thought was a nuisance. She kept her writing paper and letters and pens on top of the turntable. These had to be turfed out and dumped on the kitchen table in the middle of the room when the records were played. I would put on a 78 rev. record, put down the needle on the record, and wind up the handle with my skinny little arm. The sound which came out would be either a fast high-pitched gabble or a slow deep droning,

Granny Hodgson and my mum Vera at 104 Bilton Lane.
The vase which Bunty the budgie liked to perch on is in the background.

depending on whether the gramophone needed winding up again or not. It was great fun to a little girl. There was an interesting white flexible record with the title, 'Which came first, the chicken or the egg?' which I loved to play. It was fascinating. When my arm tired and I got bored, the bric-a-brac was dumped back on the turntable until next time.

Granny's high-backed chair by the fire, Dad's old armchair in the corner and four wooden chairs round the table completed the seating in the room. There was an obsolete treadle sewing machine just next to the cellar door near Granny's chair. Mum told me, 'Granny would sew until 2am making clothes when we were small, to make ends meet. That's what put me off dressmaking. I saw her sewing until all hours and vowed I would not do that.' That explained why Mum could hardly sew a button on our clothes when one fell off.

The cellar had a hatch from the front street for the coalman to tip the coal down. I would go into the cellar, just for a look. It smelled of coal dust and the ceiling light cast shadows in the corners of the room. I ran back up the stone steps in fear of a 'bogeyman' chasing after me.

A couple of aged sepia photographs on the kitchen wall showed Henry looking stern and military with a handlebar moustache, next to the photo of Granny in her younger days, her hair long and black then.

There was a hearthrug. When I was five years old Granny was bringing me home from school and she tripped on a wooden seed tray protruding on to the pavement outside a florist shop on Station Road. She broke her thighbone. Nowadays the shop owners would be sued, but that was unheard of then. I can remember her screaming in pain when the ambulance arrived and she was lifted onto a stretcher and put in the ambulance. In hospital a plate was inserted into her leg to fix the bones together. I asked Geoffrey, 'Is it something like a dinner plate in her leg?'

'Don't be daft,' was the reply. 'It's a long bar of metal screwed to the bones because her bones are old and they won't knit together.'

I was amazed at his superior knowledge, but thought it best not to ask what I thought was the next obvious question about knitting needles in case I got the same response, 'Don't be daft!'

She was told she would never walk again, but she did, with the aid of a stick. She recuperated at our home after her hospital stay until my easygoing dad gave the ultimatum, 'Either she goes or I go!'

After that, Granny would sit in her chair at home for hours with her feet on the hearthrug staring into the fire – 'Can you see the pictures the coal makes? That looks like a face.' Her heavy leg wore the pattern off the rug and then a hole. It's a good job the hole didn't go through further or she would have ended up in the cellar.

Mum called in to see and help Granny every day in her lunch break. By then Mum was working nearby, in the cake shop at the famous Bettys Tea Rooms at the top of Parliament Street. As I grew older I became Granny's legs and she sent me to do the shopping when I visited her. She was careful with her money and instructed me, 'Only go to one shop and then come back here.'

'But I can do all the shopping and check the change each time instead of coming back here after every shop,' I complained. But I had to retrace my steps back down Parliament Terrace each time. So I went to buy Prices candles for her candlelight in her bedroom at night (it's a wonder she didn't burn the house down), then to the butcher for some minced beef, then to Lipton's to buy half a pound of broken biscuits while my little legs went up and down like pistons as I ran up and down Parliament Terrace.

One day Granny said, 'You are very good at working out the correct change. You should be a civil servant when you grow up. That's a good job.' Servant! I had no intention of being anyone's servant and was very surprised that she would expect me to be. In fact that's exactly what I became when I left school: a civil servant.

A Shopping Trip

The Prices nightlights I buy from the ironmonger's shop in the Lowther Arcade, past Duttons for Buttons with their rows of boxes with every shape and size of button, a sample button stuck to the front of each box. I don't need buttons today so I pass by into the ironmonger's shop selling all types of hardware, their fare displayed in a melee around the shop. 'A packet of Prices candles, please,' and I clutch my rectangular maroon and white box of a dozen white wax candles as I leave the shop. The arcade opens out here into a circle where the pet shop is. I dally and watch the caged parrot eyeing the passers-by, and trying to nip an unwary and thoughtless finger. I retrace my steps along Cambridge Street past the post office on the corner opposite Wesley Chapel (where Mum and Dad were married), and across Parliament Street.

After reporting back to Granny, the purser, I have to go back to the post office to buy Granny's weekly postal order to pay for her entry into the football pools. There are long lines of customers waiting in turn in the high-ceilinged hall. Then back to Parliament Terrace with my change.

Next stop is Knowles the butcher just on the corner of Parliament Terrace and Parliament Street. I push open the heavy wood and glass door to the high-ceilinged shop. There is sawdust on the floor and a couple of women customers shuffle forward in line as if they are doing a sand dance. As I wait my turn I watch the butcher in his blue and white apron with disconcerting splashes of blood on it. His straw boater is at a rakish angle and gives him a roguish air. He deftly sharpens his butcher's knife with a swish! swish! as the blade flashes and scythes thin slivers of beef, puts them on a sheet of greaseproof paper and deposits them on the scales, placing brass weights on the counter balance to decipher the weight. The customer is then passed on to the cashier in her little glass cubicle, and the next customer shuffles forward displacing the sawdust in little swirls. This time the butcher hefts a lump of ham on the slicing machine and rhythmically pushes the blade across the meat, a pink slice curling off each time onto another greaseproof sheet held in his other hand.

My turn. 'Please may I have half a pound of minced beef?'

'Yes, young lady,' and his enormous hand stretches forward into the glass display of white dishes, surrounded by bits of parsley and meandering bluebottles, and duly serves me with my allotted amount of red minced beef, and then I pass on to the smiling young cashier and dutifully check my change.

Today I go to the Kiosk Café on Parliament Street to buy a quarter of a pound of tea. I am served by Mr Cowling, who lives next door to Granny at number 9. The bell on the shop door tinkles and I am greeted with a rich smell of coffee. There is a coffee shop here with discreet cubicles to sit and enjoy a decadent pile of cream cakes and a cup of coffee.

'Hello, Mr Cowling. I'd like a quarter of tea please.' No tea bags in those days, only loose tea grains, strained through a strainer when poured from the teapot, but which still managed to end up in the bottom of the cup or stuck in your teeth.

'Yes, love,' and his experienced hands ladle out the tea with a scoop, weigh it and put it in a sheet of paper which he miraculously transforms into a folded sealed bag in a matter of moments. I pay and off I go again.

*

Upstairs was Granny's bedroom where she had a feather bed. Mum and Dad slept there at some point, probably when he was on leave during training at the beginning of the Second World War, and he called it 'the get-together bed' as they both rolled into the dip in the middle where Granny usually slept. There was the obligatory chamber pot under the bed to avoid the night-time journey to the outside toilet. Under the window was a bath, not connected to any water, with a wooden lid on top. There was a jug and ewer on a dressing table. I didn't go upstairs very often as Granny wanted to see what I was up to, and did not trust my prying fingers and enquiring mind.

Very occasionally Granny hoisted her body and her heavy leg out of her chair and shuffled the few streets to our flat at 14 Cheltenham Parade, her stick prodding the ground at regular intervals. Then she sank into an easy chair, squinting and peering short-sightedly at our television set until she wanted to stand up again. Rocking backwards and forwards to get up enough momentum, she then propelled herself out of the chair.

She usually brought me a bar of Fry's Five Boys chocolate on these occasions, so I looked forward to her visits. The pictures on the wrapper showed a boy's face with different moods: crying, sad, wondering, smiling and laughing depicting Desperation, Pacification, Expectation, Acclamation and Realisation.

Granny ended her days with a long-term stay in hospital in a geriatric ward. Mum paid a house clearance company to take everything away at 7 Parliament Terrace. Gone were the old radio, gramophone, treadle sewing machine, chamber pot, jug and ewer, stoneware hot water bottle and sepia pictures which would be collectors' items today.

I was a teenager by then and visited Granny in hospital with my mum. When we entered the ward, rows of grasping bony fingers reached out from the lines of white beds to ensnare me. 'Come see me, come see me,' the frail voices pleaded. I recoiled from their tentacles and looked at the uniform pale faces and transparent skin, surrounded by white wispy hair, and took fright. To me they seemed menacing and threatening. I was too young and inexperienced to realise that these poor old folk were starved of human contact and very likely had no visitors of their own. But I was alarmed and kept my head down and scurried to the safety of my own grandma. I pulled up a wooden chair next to her bed, and tried to keep my eyes and concentration on her. When I retreated out of reach the other aged faces changed from their temporary animated expressions and resumed their solitary lives with resignation and blank oblivion. Their bed-jacketed shoulders slumped back into the white pillows and their fluttering fingers continued to peck at the bedclothes like sparrows pecking at seeds.

Granny greeted us by saying, 'I don't know who you are,' in a tremulous voice.

'It's me, Mum. It's Vera.'

'Vera? Is that you? And who's that? Is she a lodger?'

'No, Mum. It's Christine.'

'I don't remember her. Have I got some money in my purse? I need some money.'

'Yes, Mum. You've got enough money for what you need here.'

Mum put most of Granny's pension in a savings account, and Granny was usually aware of how much she had left in her purse. She died on Christmas Eve 1967 when she was eighty-four years old. She left no will. Mum wanted to divide equally with her two brothers what small amount of money was in the savings account. Uncle Bill said that Mum should have it all for everything she had done for Granny. Mum would not hear of it and divided it out equally. Emily must have lived with Henry for about twenty years before he died, and then she lived for nearly thirty years without him. She is buried along with Henry in a grave devoid of adornment, number 4308 Section 12N at Stonefall Cemetery, Wetherby Road, Harrogate.

The Wardman Ancestors

The Wardmans generally had long lives. There is an extract from the parish register of Fewston: '*1645 October 4th. William Wardman buried, being in the one hundred and third year of his age...*' I believe this to be accurate as there were quite a surprising number of people who lived to a great age, corroborated by the fact that they could remember national events from their childhood. Perhaps this was because they lived off the land, away from the disease in the towns.

There is one tragic exception I found. My great-great-grandfather Henry Wardman, his wife Esther (nee Needham) and their children lived in Dyke Bottom Cottage (see Appendix, 1). In December 1860, Esther Wardman, along with the youngest two of her six children, Jane aged four and Frank aged two, died from scarlet fever. What a tragedy just before Christmas. Her eldest child Thomas was aged fourteen at the time. Luckily he survived and I am here to tell this tale; Thomas was my great-grandfather. He was from a long line of farmers, butchers, grocers, weavers, joiners and craftsmen who lived in and around small villages near to Harrogate.

*

William Grainge (1818-1895) was a local historian, antiquarian and poet. He was born into a farming family in Kirkby Malzeard, but eventually moved to Harrogate in 1860 and set up as a bookseller and stationer. He was self-educated and wrote numerous books on history and topography. In his *History and Topography of Harrogate and the Forest of Knaresborough* it says, '*Blubberhouses Hall is situated to the right of the turnpike road leading to Skipton, and was rebuilt on the old site, in the Elizabethan style in 1846. During the last century* (he was writing in 1871) *a family named Wardman resided here, of whom William Wardman died in 1699, and was succeeded by his son, named Thomas, who died in 1742.'* This particular branch of the Wardman name seems to have died out but successive generations of females married into the Hardisty and Gill families. Jane Wardman was married to John Gill and they lived in Blubberhouses Hall when it was rebuilt. Blubberhouses Hall still exists and is a Grade II listed property.

The Wardman name is recorded by William Grainge as '*occurring early and continuing long*' in the parish register of Fewston. The Hardisty family '*formed alliances with the Wardmans, Wards, and other respectable families in the neighbourhood*'. I can trace my Wardman ancestors as far back as Miles Wardman de Haverah Park (between Harrogate and Fewston, see Appendix, 2) who was born in 1620 (father of Myles born 1643).

The population of Harrogate tripled in the mid-1800s with the building of a new railway station. Victorian Harrogate was a very popular spa town and my great-grandfather, Thomas, eventually moved there. He met Frances Ann Conyers at the George Hotel in Harrogate when he was working as a groom and she was a chambermaid. Thomas and Frances married on 5 November 1881 in St. Mary's Church, Harrogate and lived in a three-storey stone house, Castledine House, 7 York Place, facing the Stray and alongside the Prince of Wales Hotel, which had previously been called the Brunswick Hotel but was changed to the Prince of Wales in 1866. He was by then a cab proprietor. I wonder if celebrities who visited Harrogate, like Charles Dickens and foreign nobility, rode in Thomas' cab to 'take the waters'.

Thomas and Frances had three children: Esther, Thomas and Florence. Family history becomes confusing when the first-born son is named after the father as is often the case. There are long lines of the names Thomas, William, Henry, George and Charles etc. in many family histories.

My granny, Mary Ellen Moore, married into the Wardman family when she married Thomas Wardman (son of Thomas and Frances) at the Baptist Church on Victoria Avenue on 12 May 1906. They had three children: Thomas Conyers born on 22 September 1907; Frances Esther born on 24 September 1908; and my dad, Charles Cyril, who was born on 21 September 1909.

Grandad Thomas was a joiner who served in the Royal Engineers during the First World War where he won the Military Medal.

This is an extract from the *Harrogate Herald* on 29 January 1919:
*The Military Medal has been awarded to Sapper Thomas Wardman,
Royal Engineers, of 7 Robert Street, Harrogate, the only son of the
late Mr Thomas Wardman, of 7 York Place, for distinguished services
on the Italian front in October last. Previous to joining the Army in
1916 he was fifteen years with Mr J Checkley, builder.*

---

*In the Second Supplement
To
The London Gazette
Of Friday the 28th of March 1919*

*The military decoration was awarded to T. Wardman for acts of
gallantry and devotion to duty under fire or for individual associated
acts of bravery which were insufficient to merit the Distinguished
Conduct Medal.*

*Gazette number 31257, Military Medal. His majesty the King has
been graciously pleased to approve the award of the Military Medal
for bravery in the field to the undermentioned Warrant Officers,
non-commissioned Officers and Men.*

*Saturday 29 March 1919
Military Medal
ITALY
551142 Spr. Wardman, T. 474th Field Coy. (Harrogate)*

With that, T. Wardman earned the right to add the letters M.M. to his
name.

A sapper is a combat engineer who performs military engineering
duties such as bridge-building, building pontoons, road construction and
repair, as well as serving as infantry personnel in defensive and offensive
operations.

I have never been able to find out exactly how and why Thomas won
the Military Medal despite researching the Royal Engineers war diaries at

Sapper Thos. Wardman,
R.E., of 7, Robert St.,
Harrogate, awarded the
Military Medal.

Grandad Thomas Wardman's First World War photo.

Chatham. He seems to have been in the 48th Division and must have been at the Asiago Plateau in the Battle of the Piave in June 1918 and again at the Battle of Vittorio Veneto at the River Piave on the Italian Front in October 1918. The war on the Italian Front has been described as 'The Forgotten Front' and its importance in the First World War is often overlooked.

*

The Battle of Caporetto took place from 24 October to 19 November 1917, where Austro-Hungarian forces, reinforced by German units, were able to break into the Italian front line, and the Italian forces were routed near the River Piave. The battle was a demonstration of the effectiveness of Stormtroopers. The use of poison gas by the Germans also played a key role in the collapse of the Italian Second Army. Canisters of chlorine-arsenic and diphosgene smothered the Italian trenches in the valley in a dense cloud of poison gas. Italian losses were enormous: 10,000 were killed, 30,000 wounded, and 265,000 were taken prisoner. Thousands of artillery pieces, machine guns and mortars as well as vast amounts of stores and equipment were lost. The Battle of Caporetto was described as 'the greatest defeat in Italian military history'. The harsh Italian leader, Field Marshall Luigi Cadorna, was forced to resign and was replaced by Armando Diaz.

The bloody aftermath of Caporetto was vividly described by Ernest Hemingway in his novel *A Farewell to Arms*.

French and British troops were withdrawn from the trenches on the Western Front and sent to reinforce the Italian Front in November and December 1917. There was fierce fighting in the misty, mountainous Italian Alps above the River Piave during February and March, and again at the Battle of the Piave in June 1918 where the Austro-Hungarians were defeated, losing 60,000 dead, 90,000 wounded and 25,000 captured. According to my *Great War* magazine of 30 November 1918:

The Austro-Hungarian army had used enormous quantities of gas-shell and poured a deluge of poison over the Italian lines, and reached with special artillery all the towns and villages behind the battle-front. The Teutonic gas-shell, however, was becoming more a nuisance than a general peril. The India-rubber gas mask of the Allies was so superior to the leather protection used by the Middle Europe forces…

… The British forces under Lord Cavan were subjected to the same kind of stifling, blinding attack. The enemy rolled his artificial mists over them, filled the hollow where the railway line ran from Asiago, by Cesuna, with poison gas, and after ploughing the lines with a tornado of high explosive, sent four Austrian divisions forward like battering-rams against the 23rd and 48th British Divisions.

Austrian formations crossed the swollen River Piave, but were isolated on the west bank because many of the bridges were destroyed by barrages of artillery fire from their own troops. An estimated 20,000 Austro-Hungarian soldiers drowned while trying to reach the east bank. Lacking supplies and facing attacks by armoured units, the Austro-Hungarians were ordered to retreat by Emperor Karl, who had taken personal command.

The Italian Commander Diaz waited to press home his advantage until success could be assured. An Allied force of fifty-seven infantry divisions comprising fifty-one Italian divisions under the commander, General Armando Diaz, three British divisions (23rd, 7th, 48th) led by Lord Cavan, two French (23rd and 24th) and one Czechoslovakian division (6th), with the 332nd US Infantry Regiment, fought at the Battle of Vittorio Veneto from 24 October to 3 November (a year after the Battle of Caporetto). The Austro-Hungarian army had sixty-one divisions (about a million men) but both sides were ravaged by influenza and malaria.

On the misty night of 23 October, the Italians rowed Lord Cavan's Army across the flooded River Piave to the island, Grave di Papadopoli, and they captured the northern half of the island in preparation for a full-scale attack on the far bank. On 27 October they succeeded in establishing a bridgehead across the river, despite the river being in flood. Within a few days the Austro-Hungarian Army was routed by the Allied forces, and this victory marked the end of the war on the Italian Front. It secured the dissolution of the Austro-Hungarian Empire and the Armistice of Villa Giusti was signed on 3 November to become effective at 3pm on 4 November. This contributed to the end of the First World War. The Germans requested an armistice less than a week later (see Appendix, 3).

*

My family never spoke about my grandad and I had no idea about his Military Medal until I was researching family history, and I have no idea what happened to it. The Military Cross was awarded to commissioned officers for bravery in battle on land. Other ranks were awarded the Military Medal for equivalent acts of bravery. Since 1993 this class system has been discontinued and the Military Cross is awarded to personnel of all ranks within the British honours system.

There is a book, *Ackrill's Annual*, in Harrogate Library, which contains photos of Harrogate men who served in the First World War, the Great War, the 'War to end all wars', which of course it was not. In the book I found a photo of Grandad Thomas, the only image I have seen of him. It reduced me to tears.

After service in the First World War, Thomas became a funeral director in partnership with Frank Forrest. Thomas made the coffins and Frank undertook the administrative work. Wardman and Forrest, Funeral Directors had a workshop on Robert Street in Harrogate near the Corporation Town Yard where the council's horses were kept. I found this entry in a Harrogate telephone book:

Wardman & Forrest, Jnrs & c, back 30 Robert St. Telephone Harrogate 4510.

Thomas was not the only Wardman who served in the First World War. His cousin, Francis Henry (known as Henry) is mentioned in this sad notice in the Harrogate newspaper:

Extract from the *Harrogate Herald* on 31 January 1917

After two years and four months' continuous active service, Gunner Henry Wardman, Royal Garrison Artillery, nephew of the late Thomas Wardman, 7 York Place, Harrogate, has died of wounds received in action. His cousin Florence Wardman received a letter from the Matron of the 12th General Hospital, Rouen, on Wednesday last, saying that gunner Wardman lay there seriously wounded in the head, legs and body, assuring them that he was having every care and attention. A further letter arrived on Thursday morning saying that his condition was very serious indeed, and the doctor doubted whether he would recover. At half past nine a wire arrived stating that he had passed away. We understand his end was peaceful and that he is buried in the cemetery at Rouen. (see Appendix, 4).

The Commonwealth War Graves Commission states:

In Memory of
Gunner HENRY WARDMAN

99929, Royal Field Artillery, attd. 26th Heavy Bty.,
Royal Garrison Artillery
Who died age 45

Shandy on Sunday

On 22 January 1917
Gunner WARDMAN, Cousin of Florence M. Wardman
Of 7 York Place, Harrogate, Yorks.

Remembered with honour
Grave O. 1V. Q. 6.
ST. SEVER CEMETERY EXTENSION, ROUEN

Their name liveth for evermore.

On the eleventh hour of the eleventh day of the eleventh month of 1918 the Armistice marked the end of the First World War.

Armistice Day

In Flanders' fields the poppies blow
Between the crosses, row on row,
That mark our place; and in the sky
The larks, still bravely singing, fly
Scarce heard among the guns below.

We are the Dead. Short days ago
We lived, felt dawn, saw sunset glow.
Loved, and were loved, and now we lie
In Flanders' fields

Take up your quarrel with the foe:
To you from failing hands we throw
The torch; be yours to hold it high.
If ye break faith with us who die
We shall not sleep, though poppies grow
In Flanders' fields.

John McCrae

*

Seventeen-year-old Princess Mary had the idea of sending a personal gift, out of her private allowance, to '*every sailor afloat and every soldier at the front*' in time for Christmas 1914. This was deemed impracticable and a proposal was made for her to lend her name for a public fund to raise the money to provide '*a gift from the nation*'. There was an overwhelming response to an advertisement in the national press in October 1914 for monetary contributions towards this gift. The fund was in surplus so distribution was extended to all who were serving, whether at home or abroad, and to prisoners of war and the next of kin of 1914 casualties. Eventually more than two and a half million boxes were distributed, but there were long delays with sourcing both the brass for the boxes and for the contents. Supplies of forty-five tons of brass strip to make the boxes were lost in May 1915 when *RMS Lusitania* was sunk off Ireland on passage from the USA.

I have the 1914 Princess Mary Christmas box which belonged to Francis Henry Wardman. Depicted in the centre of the embossed brass box is the head of Princess Mary. The box still contains the two packets of tobacco, intact, and the Christmas card and picture of the Princess.

I also have his 1914 Star sent to his cousin Florence Mary Wardman, Castledine House, York Place, Harrogate, mentioned in the notice above, who was his next of kin, with the accompanying letter dated 13 May 1921:

Dear Madam

I am directed to transmit to you the accompanying 1914 Star which would have been conferred upon 99929 Gunner H. Wardman Royal Field Artillery had he lived, in memory of his services with the British Forces during the Great War.

In forwarding the Decoration I am commanded by the King to assure you of His Majesty's high appreciation of the services rendered.

I am to request that you will be so good as to acknowledge the receipt of the Decoration on the attached form.

I am

Your obedient Servant

(The signature appears to be F.A. Mitchell, Colonel.)

I also have his Victory Medal with a similar letter dated October 1921.

Another heirloom I have is a plaque engraved HENRY WARDMAN HE DIED FOR FREEDOM AND HONOUR with a note on headed notepaper from Buckingham Palace:

I join with my grateful people in sending you this memorial of a brave life given for others in the Great War.

It is signed simply *George*.

*

I wondered why (Francis) Henry was much older than many men who served in the First World War, as he was forty-five years old when he died. I discovered that he had previously served as a gunner in the Boer War:

Henry Wardman Registration number 11818
Served in the 10th Mountain Battery, Royal Garrison Artillery,
South Africa
Second Boer War 1899-1902.

Poor logistics and disease made the South African campaign extremely tough for the British soldiers who often had to go without basics such as food and water. Enteric fever killed many thousands. They had to fight a guerrilla war against a disciplined and capable enemy who were excellent horsemen and marksmen.

Initially the war was expected to be over in 1900 and medals were struck with the reverse dates *1899-1900*. About fifty of these were issued before it was realised that the war would drag on much longer than this. Therefore these dates were machined off the rest of the medals, which still faintly show the dates on the reverse side, and are described as 'ghost dated'. There are about 700 medals with two clasps left which are uncommon and desirable for collectors.

I have Henry's Boer War Medal with 'ghost dates' and two clasps stating *Transvaal* and *Natal*. It was a hard fought and hard won medal.

*

Tragically my Grandad Thomas Wardman died on 11 September 1934. This is an article copied from the *Harrogate Advertiser* after his death:

UNDERTAKER'S SAD END

HEAD IN A GAS OVEN

HARROGATE INQUEST

A verdict of suicide while of unsound mind was returned at an inquest on Thursday evening on Thomas Wardman (49) of 7, Robert Street, Harrogate, a joiner and undertaker, who was found dead late on Tuesday evening with his head in a gas oven.

The enquiry was conducted by the Deputy Coroner (Mr E. T. Heap) who sat with a jury. Mr Herbert Atkinson represented Mrs Wardman.

Ellen Wardman, deceased's widow, said she last saw her husband alive at about 6.30pm on Tuesday. He was sitting looking at the paper and listening to the wireless, and she and her daughter, who had just returned from a holiday, went out for the evening to see a friend.

Seemed Run Down in Health

Questioned as to her husband's health, Mrs Wardman said that he was a little upset at times but was alright when she left him. Generally his health varied, but for some time he had seemed run down though he had continued to work. He was, however, depressed and inclined to brood considerably over his business. He had little domestic worries, and certainly there was nothing to cause him to take his own life. He had never threatened suicide.

Mrs Wardman said she and her daughter returned home between twenty and half past nine. On opening the front door they noticed a distinct smell of gas, but could not proceed further as the kitchen door was locked. Thinking something must be wrong, her daughter went into the Catholic Men's Club and sought the assistance of Mr Vincent Bebb. He forced the kitchen door, saw what had happened, and pulled her husband out.

Burst Open Kitchen Door

Vincent Bebb, 5, Robert Street, Harrogate, club steward, said he was called out of the club at about 9-40, and at the suggestion of Mrs Wardman, burst open the kitchen door. He went through to the scullery and found Wardman with his head and shoulders in the gas oven. He was covered with a blanket. Witness turned off the gas, which was full on, extricated deceased, and attempted artificial respiration, but without success.

Dr Sinclair Miller said he had examined the body, and the cause of death was carbon monoxide poisoning. Everything else was normal.

An Old Volunteer

Well-known in Harrogate and district in years gone by as an amateur gardener, who was successful at many local shows, Mr Wardman was a member of the old volunteers, and served during the war in France and Italy. He was an enthusiastic beekeeper, and was a member of the local Beekeepers' Association. He was also a member of the Harrogate Catholic Men's Club and of the British Undertakers' Association. He is survived by his widow and three children.

He was buried at Hampsthwaite.

Grandad Thomas probably suffered from the effects of poison gas in the First World War in Italy and ill health resulted from this. Who knows what psychological trauma he endured in that terrible war.

*

My Auntie Cissie also died before I was born. She was the only daughter of Thomas and Mary Ellen, and my dad's sister.

She passed away only a few months after her father, on 6 May 1935. Granny Wardman (Mary Ellen) was in London for the Silver Jubilee celebrations of King George V and Queen Mary, and when she returned home early in the morning she noticed their chimney was smoking and immediately knew something was wrong.

Cissie's full name was Frances Esther. She was a barmaid at the Grand Hotel in Harrogate and she collapsed and died during the jubilee celebrations. Cissie's death certificate states that the cause of death was (a) auricular fibrillation and (b) mitral stenosis (see Appendix, 5). She was just twenty-six years old.

Granny Wardman

Granny sat on the stool and glanced at her three-fold wrinkled reflection in the triple mirrors, then turned to me: 'I can read you like a book.' It was one of her favourite sayings, although I cannot recall ever seeing her read a book. But I was in no doubt that she could read my mind as I was always thwarted in some childish misdemeanour. Her superior experience gained from already bringing up three children of her own was now employed on her grandchildren.

She had a warning look in her eyes. 'No you can't put on any make-up. You are far too young. Plenty of time for that later.'

'Do you mean later this afternoon? Can I have a try then?' I asked hopefully.

'No you can't, but you can watch me if you like.' Her laugh was as dry as her skin.

I pulled up a wooden chair and rested my elbow on the dressing table. My chin nestled in the curve of my hand as I prepared for my lesson in the art of make-up. Granny didn't say it was a lesson, but nevertheless it was. The bottles and jars were displayed haphazardly on a daffodil yellow dressing table set.

'It doesn't do a lot of good at my age, but you must never let yourself go. Must keep up appearances,' as she dabbed pink rouge on her cheeks with knobbly arthritic fingers. I noticed the blue veins on the back of her hands were like roads on a map meandering and branching in different directions. Next she twisted the top off a gold tube of lipstick, releasing a scarlet stick. Carefully curving a bow on her top lip, then a sweep along the bottom lip, she blotted the two together with a satisfying smack. Her eyes darted back to me and she wagged a pink-painted nail in front of my nose:

'Now don't you go using this when my back's turned.' I shook my head in wide-eyed innocence. After applying soft blue eye shadow and a covering of face powder the picture was almost complete. 'There now. Mustn't forget some scent.' She picked up the little bottle with pictures of dainty flowers on the label and the word '*Zoflora*' emblazoned in white writing on a green background.

'Mum uses Yardley 4711,' I offered.

'Yes I know, but I like this.'

Zoflora was Granny's perfume. It was a fragrant disinfectant but she liked the smell, and it was cheaper than the accepted form of perfume in fancy bottles bought from department stores. The advertising states, '*Zoflora has a much higher perfume content than is usual for other disinfectants. It kills bacteria, neutralises odour and leaves behind a quality long-lasting fragrance.*' So, because she was a non-conformist in many respects, Granny bought her scent from the chemist and dabbed it behind her ears in preparation for being seen in public.

*

As you can tell, Granny Wardman and Granny Hodgson were as different as chalk from cheese. Granny Wardman was my dad's mum. She bleached her hair using a toothbrush and neat peroxide until it resembled straw. Her favourite colours were red and yellow which she wore in abundance; not for her the greys and browns that other old ladies wore. 'I don't want to be called a pensioner, but rather a senior citizen as the Americans call their older generation,' she declared.

Her jewellery was 'poppets'. They were bright plastic coloured beads which clipped together so they made adjustable-length necklaces. Her earrings matched her necklace. I am painting a picture which sounds as if she was an old tart, but she was not. She was feisty, courageous, stoical and a survivor. She had endured the strain of two world wars and also the premature and tragic deaths of her husband and then her daughter the following year.

A Shopping Trip

She takes my hand as we skip along Cheltenham Parade: the seventy-year-old and the seven-year-old. Well, I skip and she walks, her back straight and her head held erect as usual. She tucks a rogue wisp of straw under her lemon-coloured hat. The hat matches the lemon jumper under her mushroom-coloured suit. As we embark on our shopping trip we are enveloped in a bubble of anticipation and Zoflora.

Our first stop is the delicatessen on Commercial Street, busy with morning shoppers, their bright floral headscarves reflected in the glass-fronted cabinets displaying cold meats, pies and cheeses. The apple-cheeked lady in the white overall serves us with a fresh pork pie, a quarter of haslet and a crumbly piece of white Cheshire cheese. 'And I'll have a penny duck as well, please,' Granny adds.

'Yes, love, but they're threepence now,' and the ladies in their headscarves laugh. It is a meeting place for chatter and gossip, but not for Granny today. We step out and walk through 'the ginnel', an alleyway at the foot of the bus station alongside the Baines cycle shop with colourful Raleigh bikes prominently exhibited outside. Soon we come to the little grocer's shop where we buy a pint bottle of sterilised milk. I love its creamy, slightly-caramel flavour and the distinctive long-necked glass bottle.

Granny likes to treat herself. Shopping is more fun than for Granny Hodgson as Granny Wardman shops for her little indulgences, and I get rewarded too. While Granny goes to the post office I am relied on to do another errand. I eagerly push open the shop door. The bell jangles to inform of my entrance. I take a deep breath of the rich chocolate aroma, much the same as a smoker inhales the first cigarette of the day. I don't know how the shop is decorated as my eyes are attracted to one area only. Unfortunately there are no other customers in the shop today so I can't wait in line and ogle the neat pyramids of chocolates waiting in white china trays behind the glass counter. The heady perfume fills me with longing. 'Can I have a quarter of rose creams and a quarter of violet creams, please?' I pipe up.

'Yes, dear,' as the rotund lady in her white apron picks out the meagre few chocolates with her tongs and weighs them on the scales. The rose creams have a small blob of pink icing on the top and the violet creams have a lilac dollop. These handmade chocolates are a real luxury and Granny can't afford many. My greedy eyes devour the display as I wait. Some chocolates are creamy white, some light brown milk chocolates, but I am there to buy the dark chocolates. There are different shapes, round or square, but all are in the same neat symmetrical piles.

'Thank you,' and I pay for them, collect the change and clutch the small white paper bag. The bell tinkles as the door opens again. I carefully carry my precious purchase and Granny meets me outside the shop.

'Would you like a chocolate when we get home?' asks Granny. Would I!

'Yes please.' My mouth waters. So we quickly retrace our steps home along Oxford Street past the Harrogate Theatre, down Cheltenham Parade and Granny opens her front door.

'Would you like a rose cream or a violet cream?' Decisions. I know from experience that both are equally delicious but today I choose a violet cream as I prefer the lilac colour on top. I sit and suck and savour the chocolatey smoothness and enjoy the aftertaste lingering in my mouth. My tongue searches around my teeth to collect the last remnants of joy, and I let out a long satisfied sigh.

Granny has good taste. She likes dark chocolate the best. And I like dark chocolate too, most likely from these experiences. Sometimes we bought a

Mum and Granny Wardman with Geoffrey at Poulton-le-Fylde about 1940.

bar of dark Bourneville chocolate in a deep red wrapper and enjoyed that together.

*

After the marriage of her son Thomas in June 1934 and the death of Thomas, her husband, in September 1934, and then the death of her daughter Frances (Cissie) in May 1935, my dad and granny moved away from Robert Street. She bought Linksview Café in Pannal. Dad told me that it was very popular, especially with cyclists who called in there on a weekend. Cycling was very appealing then and there were lots of cycling clubs, as many people couldn't afford cars. (The Cyclists' Touring Club of Great Britain was formed in Harrogate in 1878). Dad was living there when he married my mum in December 1937. Soon after that Granny moved away to Poulton-le-Fylde near Blackpool where she had a mobile home near a friend of hers. Geoffrey went to stay with her there for a few days when he was about twelve and Dad said he collected him from the bus in Harrogate station when he came back. At first Dad did not recognise him in his long trousers, sneakers and baseball cap. Geoffrey had gone as a little boy in short trousers and jumper. Dad said he came back as an American youth. That was Granny for you, always moving with the times.

When I knew Granny she was back in Harrogate and lived in a flat near us on Cheltenham Parade. Actually she lived in lots of different flats, but not at the same time. She flitted from one to another like a butterfly. She never could stay in the same place for a long time. I don't remember the interior of her homes very well because I wasn't often there. I don't think she was ever inside much herself either as she was out in town or at our house frequently.

Stepping out on a morning after breakfast wearing her smart suit and court shoes, she could be seen walking up to the library gardens near Victoria Avenue to feed the birds with the leftover bread from her breakfast. Never mind that most of the birds were pigeons; they were all God's creatures. She was a believer in the maxim 'Early to bed, early to rise makes a man healthy, wealthy and wise', and so she went to bed about 9.30 in the evening so she was up bright and early next morning.

She loved animals too, and when neighbours the Wood family moved away, Granny adopted their cat, so Kitty Wood went to live a few doors away

Geoffrey and Granny Wardman at 104 Bilton Lane. Granny always looked smart.

with Granny. Kitty then had kittens herself and Granny made a bed for them in the bottom drawer of her dressing table.

When we lived on Cheltenham Parade Granny would come to our house for dinner on Sundays. When we moved down to Bilton Lane she sometimes caught the bus in Harrogate town and came to see us on Saturday evenings too and we would all watch TV.

She enjoyed the wrestling matches and laughed at the showmanship and theatrical performances as the combatants threw each other out of the ring. Later in the evening Dad walked her to the bus stop for her return journey home. She was not worried about being on her own. One Saturday night, she told us, as she was getting out the key to open her front door a man came up behind her. She heard a noise and whipped round and told him to 'bugger off!' which he did rather smartly.

On Sundays, after our roast beef dinner followed by rice pudding, we would watch TV again. *Sunday Night at the London Palladium* was the highlight television show of the week for the British public. It was first aired in September 1955, in the first week of Commercial Television. The new channel was ITV (Independent Television) which was founded to provide competition to the BBC and was funded by advertisements, which themselves became famous in their own right. Tommy Trinder was the first compere of *Sunday Night at the London Palladium* in 1955, followed in 1958 by Bruce Forsyth. The show opened with the famous high-kicking Tiller Girls, a welcome from the host, a few acts and then the game show *Beat the Clock*. In the second half of the show, after the commercial break for adverts, came the top of the bill, and the finale included all the acts waving goodbye from the revolving stage. Granny loved the show, as we all did, and it was the finale to our Sunday evening before Granny went home again on the bus to Cheltenham Parade.

Granny also took me to the pictures to see the latest films. We went to the Regal on Cambridge Road in 1955 to see *The Glass Slipper*, a musical adaptation of Cinderella with the haunting waltz 'Take My Love' played throughout on a harpsichord or clavichord. The tune stayed with me and I loved the sound because it was different. In 1956 we queued outside the art deco Odeon Cinema on East Parade to see Kenneth More as Douglas Bader in *Reach for the Sky*. When pop music took the world by storm we went to see Elvis movies, sometimes at the Ritz cinema on Skipton Road. Granny liked Elvis Presley. She also liked Billy Fury from watching pop music TV programmes with me on a Saturday evening like *Six-Five Special* and *Oh Boy!*

During the daytime she liked going to the salerooms in town to buy pieces of furniture, sometimes as requests from friends. These were not always good bargains. She once bought a basket chair which was brought to our bungalow on Bilton Lane. It was placed in Geoffrey's bedroom next to his wardrobe. It was Granny's chair to sit on to watch TV in the lounge. One day Geoffrey sat in it and a leg broke. On inspection the chair was found to be riddled with woodworm, which had spread from the chair to the wardrobe. Dad had to paint a coat of woodworm killer on all the furniture and wood in the bungalow to stop it spreading. It was a good thing, though, that Geoffrey had sat in the chair and not Granny who would have fallen on the floor.

Each Christmas she enjoyed a present from Dad of half a bottle of Lamb's Navy Rum. Her cups of tea were strengthened by a hefty tot 'to keep out the cold' and as New Year disappeared, so did the rum, until a repeat performance the following year.

As she grew older Granny still continued her trips to the library gardens to feed the birds, her visits to the salerooms, and her bus rides to us for her Saturday night TV and Sunday dinner, but she was slowing down.

After New Year in 1967 Dad and Uncle Tom took it in turns to call in on her after their work as she had begun to feel the cold and they were concerned about her. I was unaware of this until one evening Tom had called round and found her dead in an easy chair. She had gone to sleep and just faded away, which was just as she would have liked to go.

When I was very young and Granny lived near Blackpool, she loved going to see the variety shows at the theatres with her friend and going to wrestling shows and just being at the seaside. But she became ill and was told she had a bad heart so she came back to Harrogate to live near her family. So it was not bad going to live to about eighty-seven years old. Dad and Tom were not really sure how old she was and I don't even know what date her birthday was. In those days we did not send as many cards as we do now so, although her death certificate shows that she was eighty-seven when she died on 17 January 1967 when I was twenty years old, I am not certain that is exactly true. I have not been able to find her birth certificate and don't know anything about her early life, so I don't know where she was born. So, despite knowing some history of the Hodgson and Wardman male lines, I am totally unaware of either of my grandmas' ancestors, as yet…

I was heartbroken at her funeral at Wesley Chapel. It was the first funeral I had been to and I sobbed all the way through. Mum put her arm round my shoulders, a rare show of affection. After the funeral I sat in the funeral car at Stonefall Cemetery at the burial and could not bring myself to go to the graveside. I had lost my accomplice in our small adventures. She was my champion when Mum said to me, 'You are not going out.'

Granny said, 'Off you go out. I was never in when I was your age.' And Mum would not disagree with her.

So I remember her positive attitude, her indubitable energy and her generosity of spirit with great affection. She was quite a character.

Bob Hope and My Mum

S hirt sleeves rolled up, sitting eating his Saturday fish and chip dinner at the kitchen table, Dad asked, 'Whatever did you do that for?' as he turned his head and stared at the milk-spattered kitchen wall.

'I didn't want to spill milk on the floor!' was Mum's strange reply.

As she had poured the milk into the teacup in preparation for the hot tea, she overtipped the bottle and a pool of milk spread onto the table. She got the dishcloth and mopped it up until the cloth was soaking, then swivelled round to dispose of it in the sink. She didn't want to clean the floor up too, but had to clean the walls instead. She was often doing things like that and wondered why we laughed at her. It was a pity that we couldn't laugh with her, but she had very little sense of humour and even if we explained she still could not understand. It's a good job Dad had a sense of humour and could laugh at himself and make light of a situation instead of being serious and cross.

'You could write for Bob Hope. I'm always telling you. I wish I knew the address of his scriptwriters,' and Dad and I laughed. Mum couldn't understand why. Bob Hope was the prolific American comedian of the time, in lots of TV programmes, radio programmes and films. Everyone knew who he was and looked forward to his shows.

In Yorkshire we did not have 'breakfast, lunch and dinner' as the 'posh' folk did, but we had 'breakfast, dinner and tea' at the kitchen table. Nobody was ever invited round for a dinner party. It just wasn't done in our circle. The most you did was have relatives round for a meal. In our case it was just Granny Wardman.

In those days milk was delivered early each morning in pint bottles and left on the doorstep by the milkman travelling round the streets in a slow motorised open-sided milk float. The gold- and silver-foil-topped bottles

66

An early photo of Mum and Dad.

were left on the doorstep and on cold mornings in winter the clever blue tits pecked through the foil tops to drink the creamy milk at the top of the bottle. The milk was layered with the creamiest at the top. People ordered as many pints of milk as they needed each day and the milkman came back, at our house, on Friday evenings to collect the cash that was owed each week.

'Where have my slippers gone now?' was one of Dad's complaints. 'It's that burglar again, I am sure. He's been in and pinched my slippers.' 'Where have you put my jacket? It's that burglar again!' Luckily we were never burgled or we wouldn't have been so glib with our laughter.

Another time Mum was sitting in her chair by the fire one evening and looking down at her sturdy legs. 'I've always had good legs. People have always said so,' as she turned them and admired them. Dad looked at me and opened his eyes wide and rolled them at me. Words were not needed, and I tried to cough to hide my laughter.

'As one door closes another shuts,' was something else I recall Mum guilelessly saying, instead of the accepted phrase, 'As one door closes another opens.'

Then there was the fire at Cheltenham Parade when Mum tried to light the wood and coal in the grate with a drop of petrol from a can. The fire was hard to light and 'drawing' it with a sheet of newspaper across the front was not a success. I was in an armchair near the fireplace when Mum threw the petrol on the fire. The flames flared upwards and ran along the liquid towards the can – 'Whoosh!' Mum dropped the can, and bits of coal spat out onto the green hearthrug and the rug caught fire.

'Quick, get out of the chair.' Mum grabbed my arm and tried to yank me sideways over the chair arm, nearly dislocating my shoulder at the same time. I erupted over the side and landed in a heap on the floor, and then Mum dragged me down the stairs in a panic. 'Mr Morley, Mr Morley. There's a fire!' she shouted. He rushed up the stairs and managed to put it out by rolling the rug up and smothering the flames.

Luckily we only lost the rug. Mum and Dad did have a row on that occasion and Dad actually swore, a very rare happening. 'Oh, you swore,' Mum admonished.

'You'd make a bloody angel swear,' was the response. Succinctly put.

Mum (in her fashionable fox fur) and Geoffrey.

Dad bought a car in December 1963 for jaunts in the countryside. We went to Bournemouth in the car for a week's holiday in 1966 and Mum said soon after we left Harrogate, 'There are a lot of people going to Bournemouth!'

Mum couldn't drive. She would have been a nightmare on the roads. It saved a lot of lives.

One 'bob-a-job' week when the Boy Scouts came round the neighbours in Bilton Lane doing little jobs and errands for a bob (shilling), Mum decided she had a good idea. She set the Scout to plant a row of potatoes in the side garden while Dad was at work. We had only lived there a few months and I was ten years old and I helped. We weren't quite sure exactly what to do, and Dad was not there to guide us. A wobbly row was dug over and seed potatoes were deposited, some upside down. We put the soil back over the top and levelled it off. The Scout got two bob for his efforts. Dad came home and Mum proudly told him of the job she gave the Scout. 'Where are they planted?' he asked as he looked at the soil which gave nothing away. 'Did you put any stakes at the end of the row?'

'I wasn't sure what to do and he didn't either,' I replied. So we had an interesting time waiting to see what came up and where. Eventually some straggly shoots appeared intermittently in a dog leg. We had to laugh. It was a success of some sort. We never saw the Boy Scout the following year, or any others for that matter. It was too much like hard work for him and he must have told his friends.

My Dad

What can I say about my dad? I loved my dad. He was fair, and kind, loyal and hard-working. He loved birds, animals and nature and could name all the types of trees. He lived by the mottos 'If a thing's worth doing then it's worth doing well' and 'You get out of life what you put into it'. He always said, 'We are a team', if he wanted me to do anything, and it worked. He would do the washing up sometimes and I would dry the dishes; if he was gardening, I would help; when he was decorating, I was there too. I always wanted to please my dad.

He was a painter and decorator by trade having worked his seven-year apprenticeship and was a craftsman decorator *par excellence*. I would say that, wouldn't I? But other people valued his work too. When he was in his fifties, one of his work colleagues, 'Ginger' Johnson, wanted to start in business for himself and asked Dad to come in partnership with him in a decorating business. Mum and Dad gave it a lot of thought but he eventually turned the offer down as Dad thought he should stay working at the Hospital Board as he had security and never knew what would happen if he was sick and was in business for himself.

Also, when he retired at sixty-five, a couple of his previous customers from Morley's sought him out and came to our home to ask if he would do some decorating for them, but again he declined because he was enjoying his retirement. He had earned it.

He was actually a very good artist but only ever sketched a few things, and he could draw from memory. He made a wonderful drawing of a pigeon, but then screwed it up and threw it away. I wish I had kept it.

He wanted to go to art school when he was young, but had to work to earn money. Together with his mate, Bert Mathers, he kept pigeons. Bert

Dad during the Second World War.

said they should only buy very good birds with a known pedigree and breed from them. He was right, and they won a lot of prizes. As Dad and Bert got older they had to give the pigeons up because they were at work and not able to clock them in after a race, and Granny had to climb up to the pigeon loft and do the job for them.

He had a motorbike and took part in motorcycle scrambles, and went to the Isle of Man TT races once, not to ride, but to watch. He often fell off his bike, and one time he crashed and was unconscious. When he came round he thought he had died and gone to heaven. A lovely young lady was mopping the blood from his eyes with her handkerchief while her boyfriend went to phone for an ambulance. The injury left him with two scars on the top of his head.

People did not wear crash helmets in those days. The Motorcycle Helmet Law did not come into force until 1 June 1973 when the wearing of motorcycle helmets became mandatory. Concern was first raised about wearing a helmet when T. E. Lawrence (Lawrence of Arabia) suffered a fatal head injury in a motorcycle accident in 1935. The compulsory wearing of crash helmets by British Army dispatch riders on duty in the Second World War came into force from November 1941. By 1973 most riders in Britain wore crash helmets anyway, but the law enforced this.

*

Dad married Mum and they lived at 1 French Street in Harrogate and Geoffrey was born on 19 May 1938. On 30 September 1938 the Munich Agreement was signed between Adolf Hitler, Neville Chamberlain, Benito Mussolini (the Italian Prime Minister) and Edouard Daladier (Prime Minister of France), agreeing to annexe a strategic part of Czechoslovakia to Germany in exchange for a peace agreement. The state of Czechoslovakia was not invited to the conference and therefore considered itself to have been betrayed. They coined the phrase 'About us, without us!' Britain's Prime Minister Neville Chamberlain returned by air to Heston airport in west London from meeting with Adolf Hitler waving the signed agreement which stated the German leader's desire never to go to war with Britain again. Today this agreement is widely regarded as a failed act of appeasement towards Germany. Hitler never kept his promise and invaded Poland on 1 September 1939.

On 3 September 1939 Neville Chamberlain made a slow and sombre announcement to the British people gathered round their radios: '*I am speaking to you from the Cabinet Room at 10, Downing Street. This morning the British Ambassador in Berlin, Nevile Henderson, handed the German Government a final note stating that unless we heard from them by 11 o'clock that they were prepared at once to withdraw their troops from Poland, that a state of war would exist between us. I have to tell you now that no such undertaking has been received, and that consequently this country is at war with Germany.*'

Britain and France had declared war on Germany. It was the start of the Second World War and Dad was called up in 1940 to serve his country. I applied for his service record while I was doing family history research. It says he did some training in Britain before being sent overseas. He served in the 5th Division, the 17th Infantry Brigade and 80 Company R.A.S.C. (Royal Army Service Corps) Infantry Brigade. His army record has a lot of abbreviations, some of which are M.E.F. (Mediterranean Expeditionary

Force), P.A.I. Force (Persia and Iraq Force), C.M.F. (Central Mediterranean Force), B.N.A.F. (British North Africa Force), A.A.I. (Allied Army Italy), B.L.A. (British Liberation Army), S.O.S. (Struck off Strength, i.e. moving somewhere else), T.O.R.S. (Taken on Regimental Strength). Some of the information states 'Unknown Destination'. I have a World War II ashtray that was made for him by another soldier. It is made from a bomb casing and is engraved with some of the places where he was sent. The places are Egypt, Lebanon, South Africa, Madagascar, India, Iraq, Iran, Trans-Jordan, Palestine, Syria, Sicily, Italy and Anzio. It is not a complete list! He told me he was in Bethlehem and it was commercialised even then. Durban was the nicest place because he liked nature and there were lovely plants and flowers there. He had a book of pressed flowers from Durban.

Dad drew this and sent it to Mum at Easter 1943. He imagined the shutters he wanted on his own home, which he eventually did at Bilton Lane in the 1950s.

He drove three- and four-ton lorries for supplies, stores and transport, and told me they could fry eggs on the mudguards of their lorries when they were in the desert. One of his mates was a hairdresser in 'civvy street' and told Dad to put engine oil on his hair to stop it drying and falling out. Some of the men could pull out handfuls of hair because it had got so dry.

They had to lay their boots upside down in the desert at night, and check them in the morning to see if any tarantulas had crawled in.

He told me these things when I was little. On a Sunday morning my parents enjoyed a well-earned lie-in after working all week. I was allowed in their bed for a while when I woke up, so I scampered into their bedroom and said, 'Tell me about the war, Dad.' These mornings were peppered with anecdotes of his war years. My eager mind soaked up these stories like a dry sponge. They had wonder, and excitement, and I still remember how they dappled the early Sunday mornings. My young mind did not understand what 'the War' meant, but he would tell me stories of pranks they got up to. But my mum did not want to hear them. It was a time when they were apart. So she turned on her side, tight-lipped, and ignored us.

Once they slowly manoeuvred a sentry box during the night so that it was alongside a nearby canal. When the soldier stepped out he fell straight into the canal. He must have been dozing. Dad said that once, when they were very hungry, they got a few supplies by going under the canvas into a lorry. In the morning their officer said, 'I'll fix the buggers!' and tied an elaborate knot in the rope which was woven through the canvas covering the lorry. In the morning he thought he had confounded the culprits but was astounded to find that some tins of food were missing and had no idea how it was done. Of course they had shuffled the rope along so that they made a gap to crawl through and then smoothed it out afterwards.

They complained there were cockroaches in the soup, but their sergeant picked the biggest one out and popped it in his mouth and ate it. Dad said that any American soldiers they met had much better provisions including tins of rice pudding, chocolate, coffee and chewing gum. He never told me any atrocities or horrors he had endured. He said he had shingles at one time, and dysentery when he was on a troop ship. The ship was full, and he slept on deck and only survived because he managed to buy some tinned pears which he could eat, but he lost a lot of weight.

He saved his army pay and sent presents home. The best present he sent was a pair of silk pyjamas for Mum and a toy train for Geoffrey. They never arrived. Parcels and post were opened and checked. Someone must have taken a fancy to the silk pyjamas.

From the *Army Veterans* website is an account of a soldier who served with the British 5th Infantry Division in Anzio which included the 17th Brigade and 80 Coy. RASC. They took over from the British 1st Division in March 1944:

The very word 'Anzio' still strikes terror in the hearts of many men who fought to hold this horrifying beachhead. 80 Coy. was transported from Salerno northwards up the coast in a fleet of DUKWS (an acronym based on D-model year 1942, U-amphibian, K-all wheel drive, W-dual rear axles) called 'duck' and shaped like a boat. These vehicles were first used in 'Operation Husky,' the invasion of Sicily in 1943. The sea was very choppy at the time, and as no keels were fitted, practically all the occupants were sea sick to a greater or lesser degree. We took over the Div. Maintenance Area which had been established about two miles from the town of Anzio and were instructed to dig in (ourselves as well as all our vehicles). As a Composite Platoon of an RASC company it was our task to collect food, petrol and ammunition from tank landing ships at Anzio docks and deliver them to trucks, split them up after working out the figures, and issue them to the various units' quartermasters, and this had to be done daily. You could set your watch by the fact that at 11am the 88s of the German Tiger tanks stationed around the perimeter would open up and we had to go to ground.

The weather gradually improved and the mud turned to dust. During April and May the forward patrols of the Brigade's three infantry battalions were limited to probing and our artillery regiments were kept busy. Stiff resistance was experienced from the German defenders. In early June the forces pushing up from the south were able to break through the defences and 5 Div. were able to push towards Rome. I remember sitting in the dug-out on the 6th June and hearing the news on a radio similar to a crystal set that the Allies had landed in Normandy. We were lucky enough to be given a day's leave to visit Rome and on that day there was a huge explosion at one of our ammo dumps.

To My Wife

Think of me, dear, when I am absent
    Send me a message to cheer my way,
Tell me again I shall find you waiting
When I come back, dear, some happy day

I'm thinking of you now, dear,
               And send this just to tell
    A little word of love to you.
From one who loves you well.

Do you often think of me, I wonder?
Somehow in my heart I feel you do!
Send a little message just to tell me
If you miss me, dear, as I miss you.

God bless and keep you, - tenderly I pray
And this my earnest prayer will ever be
I ask his blessing for you night and day,
My own dear wife, so very dear to me

Another war postcard.

From 16 January to 31 March the Fifth Army alone had lost 52,130 killed, wounded and missing. Not until 25 May 1944 was the link-up between Fifth and Eighth Armies finally achieved:

After the break-out we were sent back to the Middle East and then back to Italy again on the way to Marseilles, and up through France in cattle trucks to join the forces pushing towards Germany.

In April 1945 Allied forces began to take large numbers of German, Italian and Japanese prisoners. The Allies' advance into Germany uncovered numerous concentration camps and the scale of the Holocaust became apparent. Bergen-Belsen was liberated on 15 April, and Dachau was discovered four days later. Thousands of prisoners continued to die after their liberation because of their poor physical condition. Captured SS guards were subsequently tried at Allied war crimes tribunals where many were sentenced to death.

On 27 April the Fascist Italian dictator Benito Mussolini was captured by Italian partisans and executed the following day.

On 30 April, realising that all was lost, and not wanting to suffer Mussolini's fate, German dictator Adolf Hitler committed suicide in his Führerbunker along with Eva Braun, his long-term partner whom he had married less than forty hours before their joint suicide.

German forces surrendered and exuberant celebrations took place throughout the world. In London, crowds massed in Trafalgar Square and up the Mall to Buckingham Palace where King George VI and Queen Elizabeth with Prime Minister Winston Churchill appeared on the palace balcony to cheering crowds. Princess Elizabeth (now our Queen Elizabeth II) and her sister Princess Margaret wandered incognito among the crowds to take part in the celebrations. Victory in Europe Day (VE Day) is still celebrated throughout Europe on 8 May.

The Japanese refused to accept the Allies' demands of unconditional surrender, and the Pacific War continued. On 26 July 1945, in the Potsdam Declaration, the United States, United Kingdom and China called for the unconditional surrender of Japanese armed forces, the alternative being 'prompt and utter destruction'. The Japanese response to this ultimatum was to ignore it.

On 6 August 1945 an atomic bomb was dropped on Hiroshima. American President Harry S. Truman called for Japan's surrender sixteen hours later, warning them to 'expect a rain of ruin from the air, the like of which has not been seen on this earth'. On 9 August the United States dropped another atomic bomb on Nagasaki. On 15 August Japan announced its surrender to the Allies and on 2 September signed the instrument of surrender. The two bombings which killed at least 129,000 people remain the only use of nuclear weapons for warfare in history, yet…

At last World War II was over, but there were many years of austerity and rationing to come. There was a shortage of food, clothing and housing in Britain. The world had to be rebuilt.

My dad arrived back in Britain on 11 December 1945 after his war in Europe, serving over five years' War Service for which he was given release leave and overseas leave until 22 March 1946. He was then put on an army reserve list until 1954 when he attained the age of forty-five and therefore had no further liability for recall. He was awarded the 1939-1945 Star, the Africa Star, the Italy Star, the France and Germany Star, the Defence Medal and War Medal 1939-1945, which I still have. On release from the Army, his record states:

Charles Cyril Wardman, Army number T/236747, Lance Corporal, 80 Company, R.A.S.C. Infantry Brigade. His military conduct – 'Exemplary'. Testimonial – This man has proved himself to be a good, reliable and conscientious NCO, an excellent driver and an efficient and loyal soldier in every respect. During the numerous operations in which he has taken part he has worked unceasingly and with a cheerful disposition despite the most trying conditions. A good manager of men, he can be recommended to any employer. Signed on 8 December 1945 in Brunswick, Germany by his Captain.

I wish I had seen this when my dad was alive, but most people wanted to try and forget the horrors of war and get on with their lives, rebuilding their relationships and careers. He was just my dad and I loved learning from him and helping him.

*

He enjoyed watching cowboy films and Hitchcock thrillers. He admired Audie Murphy because he was one of the most decorated American soldiers in the Second World War, who went on to become an actor, enjoying a twenty-one-year career, mostly in Westerns. He played himself in the autobiographical movie *To Hell and Back* based on his memoirs.

John Wayne was another actor Dad enjoyed watching in films. Unlike Audie Murphy, John Wayne was classed as a 'draft dodger' because he avoided military service in the Second World War. The United States did not enter the war until after the Japanese bombed the American fleet in Pearl Harbour in December 1941, and Wayne was initially exempted from service because of his age (thirty-four) and family commitments. Many Hollywood actors did enlist, such as Henry Fonda, James Stewart and Clark Gable (Henry Fonda was thirty-seven years old and had a wife and three children). Wayne consistently kept postponing his war service until after he 'finished just one or two more films', but actually completed thirteen more movies during the war, many with war-related themes. His film company requested his military deferment, so he never fought in the war. Ironically in movies John Wayne often played war heroes as well as cowboys and cavalrymen.

Dad also enjoyed movies made by Alan Ladd and often said, 'I've never seen him in a bad film yet', but I did not always agree with him on that.

Alan Ladd was very short, at about 5ft 6ins, and always wanted his leading ladies to be shorter than he was, and very few Hollywood actresses were. When he co-starred with the cruelly taller Sophia Loren, he stood on wooden planks to appear tall, and in outdoor scenes trenches were dug for her to stand in!

Film director Alfred Hitchcock was dubbed the 'Master of Suspense' for his innovative thriller movies with a twist at the end, and we often looked for his cameo appearances in his own films. He worked with great actors and actresses of the day including Cary Grant, James Stewart, Ingrid Bergman and Grace Kelly.

Born in Bristol, Archibald Alexander Leach changed his name to Cary Grant and became one of Hollywood's greatest stars, but never won an Oscar. Handsome, debonair and charming, he could play in comedy, romance and thrillers. He was actually offered the part of James Bond in *Dr No* but refused because he only wanted to be committed to one film and did not want to do a series.

I recall watching Hitchcock's thriller *Psycho* on TV one evening with my dad. The film, starring Anthony Perkins and Janet Leigh, was shot in black and white because the shower scene would be too gory with red blood flowing down the plughole. Ugh! It was scary enough as it was.

We all loved watching comedy entertainment on TV, including Morecambe and Wise. Dad especially laughed at Tommy Cooper, the big comedian and magician whose trademark was a red fez. He was a member of the Magic Circle, but realised that he got more laughs when his tricks went wrong, so he put more 'mistakes' into his act, then threw in tricks that worked when they were least expected. Tommy Cooper had a heart attack on live television in April 1984 and died soon after.

Of course Dad was a big fan of motor racing and motorcycle scrambling and we watched them sometimes on TV in the afternoon at weekends when he wasn't gardening. We saw the exciting races as the cars roared round the circuits, jostling for position in all weathers.

Almost from the earliest days when automobiles were invented, car races had been organised. Many of the first events were aimed at proving these new machines were a practical mode of transport. By the 1930s specialist racing cars had developed. It wasn't until the end of the 1950s that full-face crash helmets were regarded as essential equipment for drivers in all forms of motor racing. But motor racing was an extremely dangerous sport in the 1950s and 1960s, and many drivers were in serious accidents or lost their lives until safety standards improved. Britain's Peter Collins, Mike Hawthorn, Graham Hill, Stirling Moss, Jackie Stewart, Jim Clark and John Surtees were glamorous figures in the racing world of the 1950s and 1960s. Peter Collins was killed in the German Grand Prix in August 1958. Mike Hawthorn was the first British driver to win the Formula One World Championship in 1958 but retired immediately afterwards because he was so upset by the death of his friend and team-mate Peter Collins. Hawthorn died in a road accident on the A3 bypass near Guildford in Surrey a few months later.

Graham Hill was another driver to survive his racing career, but then died in a plane he was piloting in 1975.

Stirling Moss survived a very serious accident in 1962 and retired from the sport and became a broadcaster, and Jackie Stewart survived a serious crash in 1966 which triggered his fight for improved safety standards.

One of the greatest ever Formula One racing drivers was Jim Clark who was killed in a racing accident in Germany in 1968. At the time of his death he had won more Grand Prix races (twenty-five) and achieved more Grand Prix pole positions (thirty-three) than any other driver. John Surtees was the only man ever to be both Motorcycle World Champion and Formula One World Champion. He died in March 2017 at the age of eighty-three.

Being a spectator was also very dangerous. In June 1955 at Le Mans, Mike Hawthorn was involved in the worst disaster in motor racing history when he braked suddenly, causing an accident where a Mercedes flew into a spectator area killing eighty-three people in the crowd, along with the French driver Pierre Levegh, and injuring nearly 180 people.

Eric Oliver was a motorcyclist and four times Sidecar World Champion, but both he and his passenger Stan Dibben retired after a bad crash in 1960. Dad would have been interested to know that I worked with Lynne Oliver at Wokingham Council. Lynne is Eric Oliver's daughter-in-law.

Motorcycle scrambling and trials riding was Dad's favourite hobby though, and after participating in his younger days, he became a keen spectator. In the UK it was originally called scrambles, and then as the sport grew in popularity, it became known as motocross racing, an amalgamation of motorcycle and cross country. We watched black and white TV coverage on BBC *Grandstand Trophy* and ITV *World of Sport*. A couple of times I went with Dad and Geoffrey, and once with my friend Christine, to scrambles meetings and we joined huge crowds watching the riders manoeuvre their bikes around off-road circuits. It was noisy, dusty and exciting watching the riders skid round corners, become airborne over the jumps, or fall off after a slide. In the 'Golden Years' of British domination in the sport BSA riders Jeff Smith and brothers Arthur and Alan Lampkin were very popular and successful, and Dad's favourites. The legendary Lampkin family live in Silsden in Yorkshire, where they moved to from London in 1940 to escape the London Blitz. They have an engineering business there. Younger brother Martin took up a successful career in motorcycling, and his son Dougie has won many World Championship trials.

*

Uncle Tom was offered a Jack Russell puppy, but couldn't really look after a dog, so he gave it to Dad. They were both soft about animals. This mischievous puppy was black and brown with big paws, so it was hardly a Jack Russell, and grew big and strong, pulling on the lead as it dragged Dad along behind. Dad called him 'Rusty' and they became great pals. Rusty was a very clever dog and learned to open doors. As I said, Dad was an excellent painter and decorator, and the varnished wooden doors in our bungalow gleamed, especially after a wipe with vinegar and water.

Rusty watched us open the doors with the handle, and close them again. He tried to copy, and jumped up and pushed the handle down, but his paws also scratched the beautiful surface of the door. Eventually he learned to jump up, put one paw on the wall, then push the handle down as we did. By then the lounge door was scratched so badly that Dad took the door off its hinges, laid it on a trestle table outside and repaired the damage so the door was as good as new.

When a carpet-fitter came to lay a new carpet in my parents' bedroom, he said to me, 'Who decorated this bedroom? Who painted the windowsill?'

'My dad. He is a painter and decorator.'

'Well, I have never seen such wonderful painting. This windowsill is like a mirror and so glossy and smooth.' Praise indeed.

Geoffrey

Vera Hodgson and Charles Cyril Wardman were married in Wesley Chapel, Harrogate. The groom's friend, Harry Hayward, was Best Man, and the bride's cousin, Mrs Edna Stephenson, was Matron of Honour. The marriage took place on 29 December 1937. Geoffrey Howard Wardman was born on 19 May 1938.

In 1940 when Dad was called up to serve in the Army and fight for his country, Geoffrey was only a little boy but learned to say, 'God bless me and make me a good boy, and God bless Mummy, and God bless Daddy in Madagascar', when he knelt and said his prayers at night.

The Government Evacuation Scheme was a major undertaking developed during the summer of 1938 designed to protect civilians in Britain from aerial bombings of cities by moving them to areas thought to be less at risk. Children living in Harrogate during the Second World War were not evacuated as they were deemed to be in a safe area, not like the civilians in London and some other major cities. Harrogate and surrounding villages were 'reception areas' for children from Leeds, London and other cities. A coachload of children were evacuated to Killinghall but misheard and misinterpreted it to 'Kill 'em all!' They were terrified.

Operation Pied Piper began on 1 September 1939, two days before war was declared, and officially relocated more than 3.5 million people, mostly children of school age, mothers with children under five, pregnant women, disabled people and teachers. Children had their name pinned on their lapel on a tag and were given a little black gas mask in a cardboard box, hung by a string around their neck. Children aged two to four and a half were allocated 'Mickey Mouse' gas masks which had large ears and were painted red and blue. They carried a bag or suitcase containing some clothes, and a bag of 'iron rations' consisting of

Geoffrey, when he was sixteen, outside Morley's Decorators.

a tin of corned beef, a tin of pears, some biscuits and maybe a tin of Carnation milk and a bar of Cadbury's chocolate. They were parted from their parents. At first it seemed an exciting trip out, but many undertook long, frightening train journeys which ended in a strange village hall and being selected, as in a cattle market, by people to stay with them. Pretty little girls were chosen first, for whatever reason, and the fit-looking boys to help on farms and with handiwork. The last children were touted round other households to see who would take them, resulting in great distress and trauma.

Further evacuation and re-evacuation occurred in June 1940 when a seaborne invasion was expected, and later after the Blitz began in September 1940. Some children were sent to Canada, Australia, South Africa and New Zealand. Many children were frightened, homesick and lonely. Some stayed with loving and kind families, but others met with cruelty, hardship and starvation. It certainly had a massive and lasting impact on a whole generation, and changed the lives of all those involved. Most of these children said later, as adults, 'I'd never do it to my kids.'

*

During the war years Geoffrey went with my mum for a while to stay at Granny Hodgson's house on Parliament Terrace and learnt to ride a bike, sometimes crashing into the wall at the bottom of the row of houses and ending up with a bloody nose and scraped knees.

After his training in England Dad served abroad and didn't come home until after the war in December 1945. Geoffrey would have been seven and a half years old but hadn't seen his daddy for about five years. Many families were in a similar position and there were millions of homes in Britain where the head of the family did not take his place at the table, and lots of Christmas Days, birthdays and anniversaries were missed. But our family was lucky inasmuch as my dad came home, or I would not be here to tell this story.

I think Geoffrey went to St. Peter's Primary School the same as I did, then to Christ Church Boys' School for two years between the ages of eleven and thirteen and then he went to Harrogate Technical College which did not take pupils until the age of thirteen. He was academically clever and also clever practically, which is not always the case. He had an accumulation of Meccano at home, a train set and a large tank of tropical fish. There was a double-tiered stand in our living room at Cheltenham Parade with a small tank of goldfish and a much larger rectangular tank of tropical fish which included angel fish, neon tetra, black swordfish and guppies. We had a piano in the 'best room' and he had piano lessons too.

Like most boys he was in the Scouts, and went off to Scout camp. When he was about fifteen he got a Saturday job at a gents' outfitters, W. E. Plummer, 6 Cheltenham Parade. In order to look smart in his job he had a new sports jacket and trousers, and in honour of the occasion Dad took his photo in front of Morley's.

Motorbikes were very popular, and sidecars too, and were often seen on the roads. When Geoffrey was about sixteen he bought a motorbike in bits which came in a large box and he assembled it in Morley's covered back yard and painted it red. Dad called it 'the red flash'. It drew admiring and surprised looks when he went out on it. It was about this time that Geoffrey left technical college and went to work at the giant English Electric Company in Bradford, and he was not home to feed and look after the fish, so the tanks were sold, along with the huge amount of Meccano and the train set. I asked if I could have the train set, but I was a girl so that was out of the question.

When Geoffrey was eighteen years old and I was ten years old my dad left Morley's Painters and Decorators and went to work at the Harrogate Hospital Board as a painter and decorator. Uncle Tom already worked there as a joiner and had been trying to persuade Dad to apply to work there as he felt it would be a better company. By then Mum and Dad had bought a brand-new three-bedroom bungalow at 104 Bilton Lane so we moved from 14 Cheltenham Parade in Harrogate town centre. The bungalow had fewer rooms than the flat, so the piano was sold.

A Triumph 1000 motorbike (on hire purchase) replaced 'the red flash' and Geoffrey used the superior machine to travel to Bradford and back. He served his apprenticeship as an engineer until the age of twenty-one and was one of the top apprentices. He worked 'fortnights on and fortnights off' which meant he worked for a fortnight on nightshift and then a fortnight on days, I seem to remember. He lived in Bradford in 'digs' with a family during the week and came home on days off and at weekends. He went to Bradford Lido on days off when it was sunny. On a Sunday when he was home, he went to Uncle Tom's at 76 St. John's Road and they spent time together in Tom's shed which was his workshop, making things and fixing things. They both enjoyed doing this and as Uncle Tom and Auntie Jessie had no children, Geoffrey was like a son to him.

In the summer after he finished his apprenticeship, he rode his motorbike on a holiday in Europe, as he was getting paid more money as a fully qualified engineer. So Switzerland and Lake Lucerne in particular beckoned and off he went with two mates. They took rucksacks and piled their gear on their motorbikes and roared off. They stayed at campsites and loved the alpine views and wonderful weather, and he brought back a cuckoo clock for Mum and Dad and a musical jewellery box for me.

In the nineteenth century Bradford was an international centre of textile manufacture, particularly wool. It was a boomtown during the Industrial Revolution and rapidly became the 'wool capital of the world' drawing immigrants particularly from Ireland and then Germany to work in the 'dark satanic mills'. Over 200 factory chimneys churned out black, sulphurous smoke and Bradford gained the reputation of the most polluted town in England with consequent outbreaks of cholera and typhoid and a life expectancy of just over eighteen years, one of the lowest in the country. Lister's Mill was the largest silk factory in the world, and at its height

Geoffrey in the garden at Bilton Lane when he was twenty-one.

employed 11,000 men, women and children, manufacturing high quality textiles. It supplied 1000 yards of velvet for King George V's coronation. Until the arrival of electric power in 1934, the mill was driven by huge steam boilers which consumed 1000 tons of coal each week. During the Second World War Lister's produced thousands of miles of real parachute silk, parachute cord, flame-proof wool and khaki battledress.

Titus Salt took over Daniel Salt and Son, his father's woollen business, in 1833, and by 1850 he had five mills and was the largest employer in Bradford. But, because of the polluted environment and the squalid conditions for his workers, he left Bradford to establish his business in Salts Mill in Saltaire by the River Aire and Leeds and Liverpool Canal. In 1853 he began to build the workers' village with neat stone houses, wash-houses with tap water, bath-houses, a hospital, library, concert hall, billiard room and school – but no pubs. By the 1980s the British textile industry was in steep decline, and Salts Mill was finally closed in 1986. Entrepreneur Jonathan Silver bought the derelict mill building and it now houses an exhibition of the work of Bradford-born artist David Hockney, together with shops and a café. There is also a film about the history of Saltaire. This model village and mill have now become a UNESCO World Heritage Site.

The huge population boom in the nineteenth century stimulated civic investment in Bradford, and there are a large number of listed buildings including the grand Italianate City Hall, the Alhambra Theatre and the Wool Exchange.

When Geoffrey went to work in the manufacturing town of Bradford in the 1950s there were still many fine Victorian buildings, although soot-blackened, and again there was an immigration boom, this time from Bangladesh, India and Pakistan. Many of these migrants found work in the textile mills of Bradford and brought their cultures with them, hence the boom in Asian food restaurants. Bradford is 'the Curry Capital of Britain'.

English Electric had two factories in Bradford: the larger was the Thornbury Works, and the smaller, Carr Lane premises. The company also had works in Stafford, Rugby, Preston and Coventry and made aeroplanes, guided missiles, electric motors, steam turbines, locomotives and domestic appliances among its products. Geoffrey was a jig-borer and made super-precision machine tools to one thousandth of an inch. Because of the work he did as an engineer, my mum hoped he would not be called up to do National Service.

The National Service Act of December 1948 extended the British military conscription of the Second World War to long after the wartime need. From 1 January 1949 all fit and healthy young men aged seventeen to twenty-one, who were not registered as Conscientious Objectors, were expected to serve in the Armed Forces for eighteen months and remain on the reserve list for four years. Men were exempt from National Service if they worked in one of three 'essential services' – coal mining, farming and the Merchant Navy – for a period of eight years. Although Geoffrey was required to do his National Service, it was deferred as he had an apprenticeship. The same happened for those in higher education. Most degree courses qualified for deferment. Six thousand young men were called up every fortnight. Most of them were not yet old enough to vote. The voting age was only lowered from twenty-one to eighteen in 1970.

After the outbreak of the Korean War in 1950, the length of service was extended to two years, and the reserve period was reduced by six months.

National Servicemen were used in combat operations including the Korean War. They also served in the Suez Crisis in 1956.

National Service was taking fit and able young men out of the economy at a time of labour shortage, which harmed the post-war reconstruction in Britain. From 1957 National Service gradually ended and the last young men entered service, and call-ups formally ended on 31 December 1960. The last National Servicemen were demobbed in May 1963.

*

Because of our age difference Geoffrey and I had no common interests or friends as we grew up. He tolerated me as his little sister, teased me too, but also encouraged me. Once, when I was very little and knew no better, he gave me a spoonful of mustard, but that's what big brothers do. On a weekend he would go off with his friends on their motorbikes, or meet in town on a Saturday night. Granny Wardman said that Geoffrey had the Wardman nose. I believe I look like my mum, the Hodgson side of the family. Geoffrey could do no wrong. He was the son and heir and my parents were very proud of him. I looked up to Geoffrey and was proud of him too.

Starting Primary School

I started school in September 1951 at the stone-built St. Peter's Primary School on Belford Road when I was nearly five years old. We did not have nursery schools or pre-schools or even playgroups, and definitely not child minders in those days. Children stayed at home with their mothers, who usually did not go to work, until they were old enough to go to primary school. I can't recall much of my pre-school years, but I do remember the incident with the matches, and also wetting Dad's chair!

We lived on the first and second floors above Morley's. There was a bathroom on the first floor, and a large living room with high ceilings, a picture rail, and an ornate ceiling rose in the centre. That's exactly what it was: a living room. We sat round the fire in winter, had our meals at the oak dining table, Dad read the newspaper and we watched TV (after the Coronation in 1953). I drew at my desk at the window, or played with my dolls on the floor, and sometimes had my bath in the tin bath on the rug in front of the fire. We still had a tin bath which I used in winter when I was very little, and I had my bath in the living room instead of in the cold bathroom. Remember there was no central heating then and the houses were cold until the fire was lit, and then it was only warm in that room. People sat right in front of the fire and got chilblains on their legs from the heat. Dad sometimes used the toasting fork to toast bread over the fire, and occasionally the bread fell in the fire! At Christmas he roasted chestnuts on the grate and they 'popped' when they were done, or you could say they exploded. In the far corner of the room was the stand with Geoffrey's tropical fish tank and goldfish tank. Looking across the road from the window we could see Herbert Wray sitting on a wooden chair outside his shop on a pleasant day. He was an antiquarian bookseller.

His books were antiquarian and so was he. Although he seemed to be sitting outside quite often watching the world go by, he must have done some business; even Geoffrey once bought a maths book for himself and a dictionary for me.

The rear of the flat boasted 'the best room', reserved only for Christmas, and was always kept clean and tidy in case we had a visitor, very rarely. Geoffrey had his piano lessons on the piano, and on the wall above were the hugely-popular three ceramic flying mallard ducks, a collector's item now. The narrow scullery glowed, painted sunshine yellow by Dad to make it bright and cheerful. The sink with a draining board was where Dad and I often shared the washing up, and where Geoffrey chopped up worms to feed to his fish. Alongside were the stove and mangle. Geoffrey fed the wet washing into the rollers, and I eagerly turned the handle to squeeze the clothes, and sometimes Geoffrey's fingers too.

The free-standing kitchen cabinet hid the dreaded cod liver oil capsules. Before school each morning Geoffrey and I had to take our cod liver oil, which repeated on us for the rest of the day. I also had to drink Ribena blackcurrant drink. I have never liked blackcurrant juice since. Before bedtime, if I had a cold, I had to eat pobs, which are pieces of bread soaked in warm milk. Pobs is an ancient recipe for poor people. The poorest bread was peasebread, made from a mixture of pea or bean flour and ordinary flour. It went stale very quickly and the only way to eat it was by soaking it in hot milk or ale. So possibly pobs is a shortened version of peasebread. I didn't like it anyway and have never liked warm milk.

As I was the youngest of the family, I had the smallest bedroom on the top floor. The cold lino floor was relieved by a pink floral rug next to the single bed where I dutifully knelt each evening to say my prayers:

> *Gentle Jesus meek and mild,*
> *Look upon a little child.*
> *Pity my simplicity.*
> *Suffer me to come to thee.*

And 'God bless Mummy and Daddy and Geoffrey and make me a good girl', before climbing into bed and snuggling under the candlewick bedspread, protected by the shepherd in the picture on the wall who watched over his sheep and me.

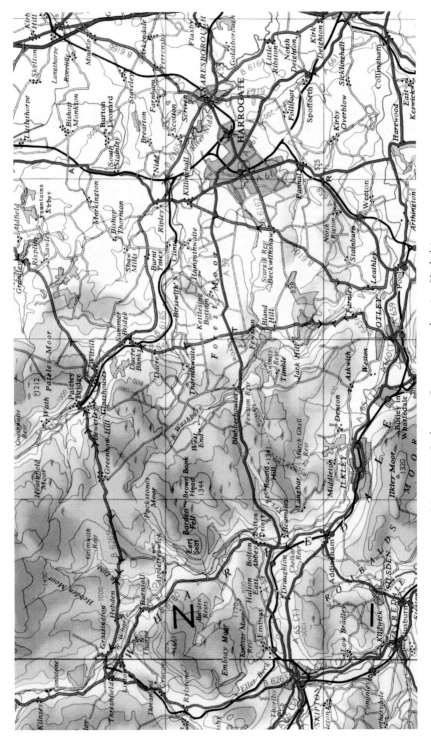

Map. 1964 Ordnance Survey map showing Yorkshire.

View from St. Mary's churchyard above Pateley Bridge.

Another view from the churchyard.

Pateley Bridge on a wet afternoon in October 2016.

The famous Knaresborough Bridge. Mother Shipton predicted that the world would come to an end when 'the high bridge had thrice fallen'. It has fallen twice.

London, Midland and Scottish Railway poster for Harrogate.

Poster promoting Harrogate as a health resort.

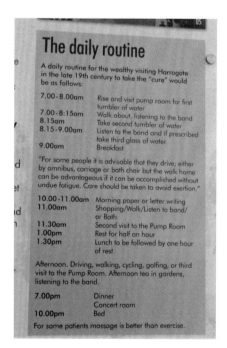

The daily routine for visitors to Harrogate in the late nineteenth century.

Hales Bar, the oldest pub in Harrogate, built on the corner of Swan Road, near the entrance to the Valley Gardens.

The Pump Room in 2016 showing the glazed annexe, which opened in 1913.

Fattorini's where we bought my engagement ring.

The Royal Baths in 2016, now a Chinese restaurant.

Inside the beautifully restored Turkish Baths.

Harrogate Theatre in Oxford Street.

The gravestone of Sergeant Major Johnston.

The magnificent Majestic Hotel.

Inside the Majestic Hotel, showing one of the stunning crystal chandeliers, and some of the classical friezes.

The Victorian gents' toilets in the Majestic Hotel.

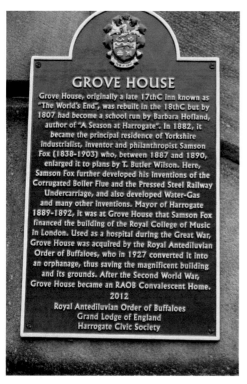

GROVE HOUSE

Grove House, originally a late 17thC inn known as "The World's End", was rebuilt in the 18thC but by 1807 had become a school run by Barbara Hofland, author of "A Season at Harrogate". In 1882, it became the principal residence of Yorkshire industrialist, inventor and philanthropist Samson Fox (1838-1903) who, between 1887 and 1890, enlarged it to plans by T. Butler Wilson. Here, Samson Fox further developed his inventions of the Corrugated Boiler Flue and the Pressed Steel Railway Undercarriage, and also developed Water-Gas and many other inventions. Mayor of Harrogate 1889-1892, it was at Grove House that Samson Fox financed the building of the Royal College of Music in London. Used as a hospital during the Great War, Grove House was acquired by the Royal Antediluvian Order of Buffaloes, who in 1927 converted it into an orphanage, thus saving the magnificent building and its grounds. After the Second World War, Grove House became an RAOB Convalescent Home.

2012
Royal Antediluvian Order of Buffaloes
Grand Lodge of England
Harrogate Civic Society

The plaque outside Grove House where Samson Fox lived.

Inside Grove House.

The Royal Hall façade. The old name 'Kursaal' can still be seen in the stonework.

Some of the boxes in the restored Royal Hall.

The Harrogate Carnegie Library with the plaque to the right of the door showing
Carnegie's donation of £7,500 towards the original building costs.

The famous Bettys Café at the top of Parliament Street.

Henry Hodgson's medals. The India Medal with two clasps showing the Tirah Campaign of 1897-1898, and the Punjab Frontier 1897-1898; the silver British War Medal 1914-1918; the George V Army Long Service and Good Conduct Medal.

Signpost along the Pennine Way in Yorkshire.

XIII

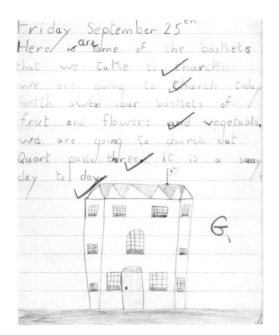

A page from My Daily Diary in 1953, age six.

St. Peter's Primary School.

Me in the garden – note the shutters.

Mum in the garden.

Me with Nellie Moser clematis at Bilton Lane.

Mum, me and Chas on our return journey from Bournemouth in 1966 with the Austin A40.

The 'cruck' wall at Dyke Bottom Cottage.

*

I started school in Miss Lee's infant class, and I remember the first day when I was a little tiddler, as we stood in rows of increasing height and years at morning assembly. I did not think of what happened to the big ones at the back of the hall. Maybe they dropped off the end as new ones started.

We didn't wear a school uniform, but all little boys wore grey shorts down to their knees and long grey woollen socks almost up to their knees, leaving the most vulnerable part of their legs prey to cuts and grazes. Boys didn't go into long trousers until they were thirteen years old. Girls wore dresses or skirts and jumpers with little white ankle socks, and little girls never wore trousers at all.

St. Peter's Church of England School is closely linked to St. Peter's Church which is on the corner of Cambridge Street near the Cenotaph (the windiest corner in Harrogate, according to my dad). More recently, the ring from the eight bells in the church tower became the first tower in the United Kingdom to have an injunction made on the bells for an offence of noise pollution!

The vicar in my day was the Reverend Roger Baines and he came once a week, on a Wednesday, to conduct our morning assembly before we each filed into our classes for the register to be taken. When our name was read out in class we had to shout, 'Here, Miss Lee', in a clear voice. We learned to recognise letters and read and write, with words like 'cat, sat, mat', and we learned to count from one to ten. At playtime a little Austrian boy in school taught us one to ten in German, so we knew 'eins, zwei, drei, vier, funf, sechs, sieben, acht, neun, zehn' too! As we moved up the classes we had to repeat our times tables every day after the register had been taken, and my tables are burned into my memory. We didn't have calculators.

Granny Hodgson brought me home from school then as my mum was working as a shoe shop assistant. This was when Granny tripped over the florist's box and broke her leg and was taken to hospital.

During my first year at school I remember a child coming back from home at lunchtime on 6 February and telling us that the King had died. I realised that it must be important because I knew about kings, queens and princes and princesses from stories about them in books at school.

At 11.15am on 6 February 1952 a black-bordered newspaper went on sale in London's streets. George VI had died in his sleep at Sandringham House and was found in the morning by Sparks, his manservant. The King was a heavy smoker and had been suffering from lung cancer and had his left lung removed the previous September, but his condition deteriorated. After his death crowds gathered outside Buckingham Palace despite the bitter cold and rain. Flags in every town were at half-mast. Cinemas and theatres closed and sports fixtures were cancelled. Princess Elizabeth, the eldest daughter of George VI and Elizabeth, was in Kenya with her husband the Duke of Edinburgh on a state visit and a short holiday at the famous Tree Tops Hotel. They flew home, arriving the next day. She was proclaimed Queen at St. James's Palace on 8 February. The King's body was to lie in state in Westminster Hall from Monday 11 February until he was buried at St. George's Chapel, Windsor Castle on 15 February after a state funeral in the chapel.

*

My first school report says that there were forty children in the class. My writing was very neat, and in art and handiwork I worked well and did very careful work. My physical training and games was good, especially running, and I should do well in sports. The final remarks are that my conduct was good: 'a very quiet child but has worked well this term'. Ha! I am not so quiet now. I was brought up hearing 'little girls should be seen and not heard', and it has taken me a long time to overcome this!

A Day Out

Six years old and going for the day to Scarborough. We didn't have a car then, nor did most of our contemporaries. This was the 1950s. The cars I saw on the roads were mostly black Fords. I called them 'back-to-front cars' because the boot projected out at the back the same distance as the bonnet did at the front. From the side the car almost looked as if it could go in either direction. Henry Ford's famous offer of 'any colour car you choose as long as it is black' summed up the market conditions of those days.

On a sunny Sunday in summer we would sometimes go on the coach for a day out at the seaside. I would wake early in the morning with excitement and rush to get ready.

Mummy and Daddy worked hard all week, so a day at the seaside was a real delight. We ate our cereal and toast for breakfast in the living room and off we set.

Have we got everything? Sandwiches for lunch, a coat if the weather changes, and don't forget the tickets. Down the road, past my Sunday school, we made our way to the coach stand. Mummy with her pretty floral dress, Daddy in a subdued jacket, shirt, tie and trousers, and me with my short dress, white ankle socks and blue sandals, skipping along beside them.

The bulbous-faced coach was already there, parked with other coaches near the Stray in Low Harrogate. The sun was already warm, and reflected off the shiny paintwork. A purple swathe of paint like the crest of a wave adorned the otherwise white coach, which was emblazoned with its identity, 'White Coach Tours'. These coach tours were very popular, and included a range of destinations: sometimes the seaside, country towns in the Yorkshire Dales or even a mystery tour.

Deciding where to sit was the next issue. Mummy and Daddy sometimes sat together, or Mummy often would ask me to sit next to her. I liked it best when Daddy sat with me. He was so interesting and pointed things out to me along the way. He was what I imagined God to be like: he seemed to know everything, was kind but firm, encouraging and inspiring, and could take me anywhere and bring me back safely home. I loved my daddy with an overwhelming devotion and trust.

On this day Daddy sat next to me, which did not please Mummy very much as she was on her own. He pointed out different buildings, and birds and trees and flowers, and made the journey pass so quickly. He was a nature-lover and knew almost every species of tree. I went on nature walks with our class from primary school and enjoyed being outside and learning about the world around me. My daddy knew so much more.

We arrived at the bus station in Scarborough, packed with other travellers, some with suitcases and others just at the coast for a day out like ourselves. The day passed in an exciting blur. We walked in the sunshine, made sand castles, and ate our picnic sitting on deck chairs on the crowded beach. Daddy gave me some money and I went to buy ice creams for us from the gaudy van, and the ice cream began to melt as I meandered back through the crowds, frightened at first that I could not find my mummy and daddy.

Eventually, tired and happy and with the shadows lengthening, we made our way back to the coach and our comfy seats. I fell asleep on the way home and Daddy laughed at me with my head back and my mouth wide open, and I stirred and laughed too. What a great day, something to write about in 'My Daily Diary' at school the next day.

*

Still in the infants in my second year at school we practised our writing in an exercise book called 'My Daily Diary'. My language skills were not well developed yet so all I wrote was 'Yesturday we went to the seeside.' The weather chart on the wall was completed each day by a different child who drew a picture of an umbrella, or snow, or sunshine to record the day's weather. Reading My Daily Diary it states that it was a 'dull day' quite often.

The Great Smog in London came in December 1952. Cold weather meant that Londoners were burning more coal than usual to keep warm which led to the severe air-pollution event. Post-war domestic coal tended to be relatively low-grade, and sulphurous, which increased the sulphur dioxide in the smoke. There were also numerous coal-fired power stations in the Greater London area. Prevailing winds had also blown heavily-polluted air across the English Channel from industrial areas of Continental Europe. Pollution and smoke from vehicle exhaust, from steam locomotives and also diesel-fuelled buses, which had replaced the recently abandoned electric tram system, all added to the 'peasouper', so called because the tarry particles of soot gave the smog its yellow-black colour. On 4 December an anticyclone settled over a windless London with cold stagnant air trapped under a 'lid' of warm air. Visibility was down to a few yards. Public transport stopped, except for the London Underground. The ambulance service stopped too, and sporting events, and concerts and film shows were cancelled because the smog even seeped indoors. At the time it was estimated that 4000 people had died prematurely in December and 100,000 were made ill because of the smog's effect on the human respiratory system. More recent research suggests that the total number of fatalities was considerably greater, at about 12,000. The Great Smog is known to be the worst air-pollution event in the history of the United Kingdom and led to the Clean Air Act of 1956 to reduce air pollution by switching to electricity, gas and coke, and relocating power stations away from cities.

I remember smogs in the 1950s and early 1960s even in Harrogate when you could taste the smog and visibility was down to a few yards. People wore scarves over their mouths, and it was disconcerting not knowing exactly where you were and maybe bumping into someone walking towards you. You could hear muffled footsteps around you but could not quite discern where they were coming from.

During that school year, at the end of January 1953, the North Sea flood happened, one of the most devastating natural disasters ever recorded in the United Kingdom. Whole families died, 24,000 homes were damaged in the UK and 47,000 farm animals were drowned. The ferry Princess Victoria, which sailed twice a day delivering mail and ferrying passengers, was sunk in the North Channel between Scotland and Northern Ireland with the loss of 133 lives. Fishing boats were sunk. Over 2500 people were killed on land and at sea in Scotland, England, Belgium and the Netherlands. A combination of a high spring tide and a severe windstorm over the North Sea caused a storm tide. The sea rose over eighteen feet in some places. Floods overwhelmed sea defences. The low-lying Netherlands was worst affected where dykes were breached and over 1800 deaths were recorded and widespread property damage occurred.

At the time, no local radio stations broadcast at night. As the disaster struck on a Saturday night, many government and emergency offices were not staffed. Most people did not have telephones, and these were disrupted by the floods anyway. So, as the floods moved down the east coast of Britain and then funnelled down in to the Netherlands (much of which is below sea level), there was no warning and people were unable to make preparations. Many people died in their beds on the east coast of England and in the Netherlands as the wall of water surged relentlessly on.

Coastlines and properties in Scotland and the east coast of England were badly damaged and in Lincolnshire the floods reached two miles inland. People climbed into their lofts and onto roofs in the pitch black in the middle of the night to escape the rising waters, and it was not until the light of morning that the devastation became apparent.

The event has more or less disappeared from history because Britain wanted good news after six rigorous years of the Second World War, and the

Butlins, Filey, 1953. I am the little girl peeping out on the left next to Geoffrey, with Mum and Dad opposite.

disaster affected mostly poor families who lived in coastal areas, sometimes in prefabricated houses erected after the war because of housing shortages. As a result of the North Sea Flood of 1953 ambitious flood defence systems were constructed. The Thames Barrier programme was started to secure central London against a further storm surge, and the Thames Barrier was opened on 8 May 1984.

Good news was on its way, though. Sir Edmund Hillary and Sherpa Tenzing became the first men to reach the summit of Mount Everest on 29 May and the news reached Britain on 2 June 1953, the day the Coronation of Queen Elizabeth took place in Westminster Abbey. This date was chosen for the coronation as records showed it was the most likely day to be dry. It poured with rain. The coronation of the Queen was the first ever to be televised and many people in Britain bought television sets especially for the event, my family included. The young Queen wore the heavy Imperial State Crown and her dress was designed by Norman Hartnell. Richard Dimbleby, whose eldest son David now commentates at national events and elections, commentated for the BBC as we watched the flickering black and white pictures of the ceremony on our TV. We were all given commemorative cups at school. Geoffrey had a blue beaker and mine was a small cup with a gold rim. Both were broken over the years.

In my report at the end of the school year in July 1953 Mrs Davies wrote that there were now forty-five children in the class. My report is peppered with 'Very good', 'Well done', 'Very keen', 'Christine enjoys her singing, games and rhythmic work' and the remarks at the end say, 'Christine is a very neat worker. She works hard and steadily.' I am bragging, aren't I?

In the school holidays that year our family went to Billy Butlin's Holiday Camp in Filey. We didn't have many holidays so this was a treat. We stayed in chalets and ours was near the end of a row and the loudspeaker nearby woke us all up in the morning with its 'Wakey, Wakey' call. (Band leader Billy Cotton started his BBC TV show *Billy Cotton's Band Show* with the band's signature tune and Billy's call of 'Wakey, Wakey' taken from Butlins.)

Our meals were taken in huge dining rooms with long rows of tables, and entertainment was provided by Butlins Redcoats. I can't remember much about the holiday but I do remember you could make a request to be played on Radio Luxembourg when it was your birthday. I requested 'In a Golden Coach', a song about the Queen's coronation which was popular at the time and sung by Dickie Valentine. When my birthday arrived we listened to the programme on our big radio (the one Geoffrey had hidden the matches behind), and it was played.

*

Mrs Gill was my class teacher in my third year from September 1953 to July 1954. In the autumn of 1953 Myxomatosis reached the UK from Australia and Europe, and I can remember reports on the news. It was estimated that there were about 100 million rabbits in Britain and Myxomatosis was encouraged as a means of rabbit control. It caused the rabbits great distress with skin tumours, blindness, pneumonia and death, usually within fourteen days. This was quite shocking as we in Britain were brought up on stories of Peter Rabbit by Beatrix Potter. But rabbit was a staple food in Britain during the war years because it was a cheap, lean and nutritious meat. Many people kept rabbits and chickens to supplement their meagre meat ration. Rabbit tastes similar to chicken, but has lots of small bones. At least 95% of rabbits in the UK were killed by the Myxomatosis outbreak but have increased greatly since as a result of genetic resistance or acquired immunity. Rabbits again now cause damage to farmers' crops, and burrow under roads and railways causing subsidence, and chew through the bark of trees which prevents the regeneration of woodland. Vandalism by rabbits is estimated to cost the British economy at least £100 million a year. But the habit of eating rabbit is not popular nowadays.

We did our sums in pounds, shillings and pence. Decimalisation was not introduced in the UK until February 1971, so we learned that a pound was made up of 240 pence, there were twelve pence in a shilling and twenty shillings in a pound. That was £ s d. The letter d was for the Latin '*denarius*' and the penny is now referred to as the 'old penny'. We also worked out our measurements in yards, feet and inches: twelve inches in a foot, and three feet in a yard, therefore thirty-six inches in a yard. At playtime we played ball, or skipped, or played 'tag' in the playground. At Harvest Festival my dad decorated a basket for me and we filled it with fruit and vegetables for me to take to St. Peter's Church. On Bonfire Night he set off a few fireworks on the wall in the back street and we held sparklers. That was the extent of our Bonfire celebrations, but there were many accidents in people's back gardens which led to the big public firework displays instead of many private shows.

I made paper chains each Christmas and Dad hung them from the corners of the living room to the centre light. Our artificial tree came out

My school photo, age eight, after Mum used the curling tongs.

My school photo, age nine, different hairstyle, same jumper.

each year with the perennial decorations and it was my job to decorate the tree. Although earlier artificial Christmas trees were developed in Germany and made of goose feathers dyed green, modern trees were made of brush bristles. In 1930 British-based Addis Housewares Company created the first artificial Christmas tree using the same machinery that was used to make toilet brushes, then dyed the bristles green!

As Christmas neared Mum asked what I would like from Santa. We were out shopping in the Lowther Arcade and I showed her the doll dressed as a bride and another doll in a Scottish tartan which I admired in the window. On Christmas morning I found my usual packet of liquorice which included laces, a pipe and Catherine wheel. Then I delved into my dad's woollen sock which had been left at the foot of my bed. There was a tennis ball, some sweets and the usual tangerine right at the bottom. (Tangerines were always full of pips and we only had fruit and vegetables in season in the shops.) Rushing downstairs to the living room I found two parcels: one was the bride doll and the other was the Scottish doll. I was amazed how Santa knew just what I wanted!

My reading and writing were progressing well. One January day I have written in My Daily Diary, '*It is the coldest day for six years. Donald has done the weather chart. I have a loose tooth. There were icicles on Tony's window this morning. Sandra saw a milk bottle full of ice and the milk was frosen. Mr Bainbridge was sliding on the ice at playtime. We had Bank this morning.*' On Tuesdays I brought in 1s 6d to put in our bank book for the Yorkshire Penny Bank, later to become the Yorkshire Bank.

Before the First World War all bank staff, including typists, were male. A few women typists were then employed as an experiment, mainly because they could be paid less than men. During the First and Second World Wars there was a staffing crisis and women were employed, mainly on a temporary basis and paid a weekly wage, to fill the jobs of men who had gone to serve in the wars. Some women were kept on, but had to resign if they got married. Although salaries at the beginning of a banking career might be broadly similar for both men and women, men's salaries rose more rapidly. This was rationalised by the assumption that men would marry in their twenties and become responsible for supporting a family, whereas women would be single and therefore did not need as much money! Because of staff shortages after the end of the Second World War, several banks offered their female staff gratuities to keep their jobs. From 1950 banks gradually removed the marriage bar which had forced women to resign from the bank on marrying. There had been a similar marriage bar in teaching and the Civil Service and some large companies. Married women had been expected to remain at home and look after their husbands and children: 'No woman should hold two positions. They cannot serve two masters.' But times were changing.

The Grove Family came into our homes courtesy of BBC Television in April 1954 and we followed the life of the family in this first British soap opera on our new television until the series ended in 1957. I also watched *Muffin the Mule*, a puppet character presented by Annette Mills, sister of actor John Mills, and *Andy Pandy*, *Sooty* and *Bill and Ben, the Flower Pot Men*.

On 6 May 1954 Roger Bannister became the first person in the world to run the mile in under four minutes. It was achieved at the track of the University of Oxford with Chris Chataway and Chris Brasher as pacemakers. The weather was not ideal for the record-breaking attempt, with a crosswind and strong gusts which nearly caused the attempt to be called off. Pandemonium broke out when the spectators heard the result being announced. It was a great sporting landmark.

In July 1954 my school report by Mrs Gill included a couple of 'excellents' as well as 'very goods', 'reads fluently' and 'Christine has worked quietly and steadily in this class and made very good progress.'

The Mid-1950s

Our teacher in Class 4 was Mr Rowntree and he gave us the 'bumps' when it was our birthday. He swung us round a few times and then gently bumped us on the floor. We all enjoyed it, but it would not be allowed nowadays. I had school dinners because my mum was working, but some children went home if they lived quite close. Our lunch break was an hour and a half and the whole school day was from 9am until 4pm with a fifteen-minute playtime morning and afternoon. The dining room was in a building on Victoria Avenue just around the corner from the school, and we lined up and walked in crocodile fashion to eat our meal at tables which seated about a dozen of us. We had to eat whatever we were given because there were starving children all around the world, we were told. If we left food on our plates we were chastised, so we started to pile the plates at the end of the table with all the food squashed in between each plate. Mr Bainbridge would not allow this and he inspected each plate, so then children started throwing food under the table, and this was noticed too and Mr Bainbridge was furious. Susan cried as she did not like mashed potato, so I ate hers. We all hated soggy boiled cabbage, tapioca and semolina. The thought makes me cringe now. I went to tea one day at Susan's house and her mum gave me cabbage. I didn't want to say that I did not like it and started to eat it as I had always been told. To my great surprise it was very tasty, so I don't know what they did with the school dinners.

Granny Wardman waited in our house for me coming home from school as, by now, I was allowed to walk home without an adult. My friends and I went to the sweet shop on Commercial Street on the way home and we bought four chews for 1d, or a gobstopper, or bubble gum. 2d or 3d went quite a long way. David Fisher was in my class and, despite the surname, his family had a butcher's shop on Commercial Street. Helen Solk was in my class too, and her Jewish family had a grocer's shop in the street. I remember the shelves full of tins and jars in the storeroom behind the shop, filled with Carnation milk, Camp Coffee, Robertson's marmalade and bags of flour. One day we sat on a wooden box eating a pomegranate, picking each seed out with a pin. I had never seen a pomegranate before and didn't realise until many years later the symbolism of pomegranates in ancient cultures. It is mentioned or alluded to many times in the Bible, and some Jewish scholars believe the pomegranate was the forbidden fruit in the Garden of Eden. Pomegranates are traditionally eaten on Rosh Hashana, or Jewish New Year, as they symbolise fruitfulness or fertility.

Brown's department store, on the corner of Commercial Street and Bower Road, used a 'cash ball' system to carry the cash from the sales counter up to the cashier's office, and the change dispatched back down to the customer. I watched in wonder as the salesperson put the money in the hollow ball and sent it on its way on the track above our heads, and then we waited for the change to be returned on a different track and drop back down to the counter. I believe the system is still demonstrated at Beamish Museum in County Durham.

I was often in trouble for dawdling home with my friends, or wearing holes in my knickers by sliding down the concrete air raid shelter which still stood down the alleyway at the side of Woolworths. One day I fell off a wall and bloodied my nose and bashed my front teeth. A man cycling past saw me fall and took me home where I received little sympathy and much scolding. I was in trouble too for not going to Sunday school, which was the Wesley Chapel Sunday School at the bottom of Cheltenham Parade, the date of its opening engraved in stone above the door: 1873. As intended, the date is still there today, but the building is now, surprisingly, an Indian restaurant with a doorman in Indian garb to open the door and usher customers inside. There are feature walls of cascading water, next to brown tables and brown leather seats. In the 1950s the Sunday school was made up of a central row of chairs, a stage, and cubicles for classes at the sides of the hall, and a gallery above. It is unrecognisable now.

Mum primly informed me, 'When we were young I had to go to Sunday school with Fred and Clarence,' (she always called him Clarence and knew he hated it) 'and we went hand-in-hand three times a day on Sundays, morning, afternoon and evening.'

So I dutifully went off down Cheltenham Parade on Sunday afternoons while my friends played outside on Mount Parade. I got a prize of a book for very good attendance initially, but my interest waned, so I started off to Sunday school, but then walked right past, turned the corner and up the back street to Mount Parade to play with my friends. We chalked numbered squares on the pavement outside Mrs Jackson's and played hopscotch. There was a beautiful tree in her garden, dripping with lemon yellow flowers. It was a laburnum tree, and I was reliably informed by my friends that it was poisonous, as was Mrs Jackson. She always came out of her house to tell us off. 'Don't chalk on the pavement. Go away and play somewhere else.' So we slunk off, only to return a while later. Why we didn't chalk our hopscotch game somewhere else, I have no idea. We were perverse. So we carried on playing, in fear that Mrs Jackson would storm out, drag us in, hit us with a rolling pin, tie us to a chair and force us to eat laburnum flowers.

This happy situation couldn't last. I stayed playing too long and too often. I returned home late because I didn't know what time it was, to be greeted with the question, 'Where have you been?' in an accusing manner by my mum.

'Sunday school,' I replied in wide-eyed innocent wonder.

'No you haven't!' and I was subjected to a tirade which ended, 'and you won't go to heaven.'

I was still getting good school reports, though. Mr Rowntree wrote, 'A very neat and careful worker. Expression work good, and always in the top group.'

That summer Uncle Bill, Auntie Freda and cousin John came to stay with us for a week, then took me home on the train to stay with them in Deal in Kent. Uncle Bill used to work as a gardener at Harewood House and they had lived in Harrogate not far from us. He was very good at mental arithmetic and could work out quickly how many plants were needed for a display bed. When the position of a cemetery and parks superintendent became available in Deal, he applied for it and became the youngest superintendent in the country. So they moved to Deal and lived in the house in the grounds of the cemetery. I spent three weeks' holiday with them away from the restrictions at home and enjoyed the seaside. The weather was lovely and John, who is a couple of years younger than me, had Weetabix-eating competitions with me and then we played outside in the sunshine. Auntie Freda had a pressure cooker, but the meals were not always a success as they sometimes ended up on the ceiling. I learned to ride a bike, fly a kite near the seafront, and we had picnics on the pebble beach where we could still see wrecks of ships on the notorious Goodwin Sands just off the coast. There have been numerous wrecks and many lives lost on the shifting sands which are exposed at low tide then quickly submerged as the tide comes in. At low tide the sands are firm enough to stand on and in recent times the well-known cricket matches are played there.

The lawn next to the house in Deal had a little putting green and we tried to play golf. In the evenings I was allowed to read books until the light faded and the sky beyond the leaded lights on the windows began to darken. It was a lovely holiday, and then my parents and Geoffrey came for a few days' holiday themselves and took me back home on the train again.

I played out during the rest of the holidays and often went to the swings at the Rose Gardens, scuffing my shoes again. Although my mum worked in a shoe shop, I don't think I got new shoes until my toes were cramped. Shoe shops used x-ray machines, known as Pedoscopes, and kids loved looking down through the viewer at our toes wiggling in the shoes. There were no health regulations then regarding these machines. The radiation dose was directed at the feet, but there were leaks to the rest of the body, and sales staff were exposed to the radiation daily. Children are about twice as radiosensitive as adults. Eventually the health hazards of radiation brought in stringent regulations which forced the gradual phasing out of Pedoscopes. So it was perhaps fortunate that I did not go often to have new shoes, but my cramped shoes did leave me with a bunion on my left foot.

When I went out to play my mum always wagged her finger at me and told me not to talk to any strangers nor take sweets from anyone. Yet when she was at work and I was at home in the holidays she arranged with Mr and Mrs Entwistle that I would go to the café above their grocer's shop for lunch at 8 Cheltenham Parade. So I sat upstairs on a bench, the only little girl, squashed up with all the workmen who came for their lunch. Although she was a bit older than me, I played with their daughter Kathleen and her cousin John who I met again a few years later when we moved to Bilton and he played at Bilton Cricket Club. I went to John's wedding when he married Ann in September 1966. They had their Golden Wedding in 2016.

*

In September 1955, when I was almost nine years old, I went into Miss Dunkley's class and we started to sew and knit and, as usual, my work was very neat. We made school scarves for the winter. As our writing improved we used ink and fountain pens and there was an ink monitor who went round the class filling the inkwells each day. We didn't use ballpoint pens then at school. Nowadays ballpoint pens are mass-produced cheaply all over the world and are usually called biros after Laszlo Biro, a Hungarian newspaper editor who filed a British patent in June 1938 for his innovative commercially-viable ballpoint pen. He was frustrated with filling up fountain pens, and cleaning up smudged pages, and noticed that inks used in newspaper printing dried quickly. So, with the help of his brother Gyorgy, a chemist, he produced a ball-socket mechanism with an ink which flowed evenly without drying in the chamber.

After school I watched TV. I often watched a BBC children's television series called *Crackerjack*, first introduced by Eamonn Andrews. Our set had a fourteen-inch screen, but smaller ones were available – nine-inch and twelve-inch sets. The TV was a cumbersome piece of furniture with a large cathode ray tube protruding from the back of the set. The picture looked as if you were in a car in a snowstorm, but without windscreen wipers. Every now and then, just at the interesting part of a programme, the picture started to roll, and Dad had to adjust the horizontal hold by turning a knob at the back of the set. If the picture started to roll again, he banged the side of the TV. That stopped it for a while, until off it went again. We didn't have leisure centres in those days; we didn't need them. We got all our exercise jumping up and down to realign the picture on the TV.

There was a new channel now called ITV, launched in September 1955, which was the Independent Television Authority, as well as the BBC. There were no remote controls then, so we had to jump up from our seats to change the channel too. We received ITV courtesy of Emley Moor. Emley Moor is not a person but a transmitting station west of Emley, Kirklees, West Yorkshire, which provided ITV broadcasts to the Yorkshire area. The 135-metre lattice tower was built in 1956, transmitting Granada TV programmes on weekdays and ABC TV programmes at weekends, providing limited coverage. Its performance was improved in anticipation of colour transmissions in 1966, when a 385-metre guy-supported tubular mast was erected, which was one of the tallest standing structures in the world at the time. The mast was regularly coated in ice during winter, and large icicles formed on the guy wires. On 19 March 1969 a combination of strong winds and ice which had formed around the top of the mast and on the guy wires brought the structure down, leaving several million people without a service. Some service was restored within four days by a collapsible emergency mast. The present 330-metre concrete tower, the tallest freestanding structure in the UK, was started nearby in 1969 and became operational in January 1971.

The BBC had intervals between programmes and showed short films to fill up the gaps or as a standby in case of a studio breakdown, which was quite often. The most popular interlude films were *The Potter's Wheel* and *Angel Fish*, accompanied by peaceful music. The test card was shown, usually at start-up before actual programmes were broadcast and at close-down. It showed a set of geometric shapes and patterns to enable TVs to be calibrated and adjusted to show the picture correctly. Of course the picture was all in black and white so there were just different shades of grey. We had an H-shaped aerial on the roof to receive the signals. Programmes only ran for a few hours each day with a break after children's programmes between 6pm and 7pm so that parents could put the children to bed – 'the toddlers' truce'. We sometimes ate fish fingers for tea, a new revelation introduced by Clarence Birdseye, followed by banana and custard or tinned fruit, before programmes started again in the evening. We were advised to watch TV with the main light in the room switched off, and view the TV with the light from a small table lamp. Burglars learnt that if there was a dim flickering light from a window, then the occupants were all gathered in one room peering at the TV. They could slip in the front door, burgle the house and slip out again without anyone noticing.

We watched Jack Warner as *Dixon of Dock Green*, and panel games like *What's My Line?*, Johnny Morris on *Animal Magic*, the science-fiction *Quatermass*, and *Come Dancing*, which is the very early version of *Strictly Come Dancing*. Our evening TV viewing was often disrupted by Mr

MacEwan, who worked at the dental laboratories next door at number 16. He made dentures in the evenings and the electric machine he used interfered with our television reception and made the picture snowier than usual, and unviewable. I went to bed about 7.30pm so I did not see the late evening programmes or the National Anthem being played at the end of transmissions for the day. When the TV was switched off a white dot appeared in the centre of the screen and then faded away.

I often caught colds. There was actually a Common Cold Unit set up in 1946 near Salisbury which was intended to find a cure for the common cold which accounted for a third of all acute respiratory infections and a substantial number of days off work. Thirty volunteers were required every fortnight for an all-expenses-paid stay in the Salisbury countryside. The advert for volunteers ran, 'Free 10 day autumn or winter break. You may not win a Nobel Prize, but you could help find a cure for the common cold.' Journalist puns described the trial as a 'holiday not to be sneezed at' with 'cold comfort provided', because these volunteers were infected with common cold viruses. Actually only a third of the volunteers on any trial were administered with a cold virus; the others were given a placebo, and a lot of people did treat it like a holiday, or did their dissertation for university in peace and quiet. Dr David Tyrrell was the head of the CCU and discovered how and why colds were transmitted, and also discovered that colds were caused by hundreds of different viruses and that it was impossible to vaccinate against each of them. By the time the unit closed in 1990 over 20,000 volunteers had taken part in the cold trial, but no cure for the common cold was found, so I still had to suffer like everyone else and hope that chicken soup helped alleviate the symptoms. Dr Tyrrell became involved in the work of the World Health Organisation and then HIV/AIDS and more deadly diseases.

*

On Thursday evenings my mum and dad cleaned the shop and office downstairs and I helped. Wallpaper rolls were not covered in cellophane then, but had selvages to protect the edges of the wallpaper, which were then trimmed off by cutting wheels before wallpapering the walls. Morley's had a big wooden trimming machine which cut off the edges, and my job was to clean out all the long spirals of edging paper. After helping I was allowed to sit at secretary Miss Hebblethwaite's desk (what a wonderful Yorkshire name) and telephone upstairs to our flat and speak to my dad.

Life was changing in Britain. Music was beginning to liven up from the crooners who sang gentle ballads. Bill Haley's recording of 'Rock Around the Clock' was a number one hit song in the USA and the UK in 1955 and became the biggest-selling UK single of the fifties. It was a revelation to young people. Rock 'n' roll had arrived! It was raw and exciting!

In July racing driver Stirling Moss had become the first English winner of the British Grand Prix at Aintree Motor Racing Circuit. Unemployment in the UK was less than 1%. Rationing had finally ended in Britain in 1954 and supermarkets were becoming popular. Introduced from America, they were called self-service shops in Britain, and tempted the shopper with an increasing array of food on the shelves from which to choose. Convenience foods such as pre-packaged cake mixes became popular – a rather odd choice. New and exotic imports including garlic, pizza and spaghetti, and new varieties of cheeses were stacked on shelves. Supermarkets began selling alcohol, which had only been sold in off-licence stores previously. Sliced bread had been invented in 1928 in the USA, and commercial bread slicers for use in large bakeries were introduced in Britain in 1930. Until then all bread was sold in whole loaves and had to be sliced at home, resulting in uneven slices and cut fingers. My mum had a bent and damaged index finger on her left hand from cutting a loaf of bread, so when she wagged her finger at me she was pointing the wrong way.

Sliced and wrapped loaves were prohibited during the Second World War as an economy measure, but were reintroduced in 1950. The fortification of flour in the UK became established in the 1950s. In 1941 calcium had been added to flour to combat rickets, followed by the restoration of iron, Vitamin B1 (thiamine) and niacin, which had been lost in the milling process. New soap powders such as Daz, Tide, Omo and Persil were all supposed to wash whiter in the new washing machines, but most of the powders were made by the same company and just went out of a different door in the factory. Advertisers advised us to 'go to work on an egg' because they are highly nutritious and provide significant amounts of vitamins and minerals. We sometimes had double-yolkers then, before our eggs were graded into different sizes. Our modern staple, yoghurt, was not launched in the UK until the Swiss company Ski launched their product here in 1963. With added sugar and real fruit it was an instant hit, and was a revolution on our supermarket shelves. Today yoghurt is revered as a functional superfood, claiming a number of health properties. Where would we be now without yoghurt to give to our children and grandchildren?

*

All children looked forward to the weekend when we went to 'Saturday morning pictures'. My friends and I usually went to the ABC Regal Cinema on Cambridge Road and we all jostled outside before it opened, then rushed and pushed our way in to pay our 6d entrance fee. That was until we found out we could get in free by waiting outside at the emergency exit. A couple of our friends paid to get in and then pretended to go to the toilet near the emergency exit and pushed the bar to let the rest of us in and then we spent our money on sweets and shared them out. The staff got wise to this and waited along the corridor to catch children, so that did not last long. We were able to use the push-bar exits because of a disaster.

The Glen Cinema Disaster in Paisley on the afternoon of New Year's Eve 1929 caused the deaths of seventy-one children and injured forty more. During a children's matinee, a freshly-shown film was put in its metal can, where it began to pour out thick black smoke. Soon the smoke filled the auditorium containing about 1000 children. Panic set in and the children stampeded downstairs so fast that they piled up behind the escape door. The door could not be opened as it was designed to open inwards, and it was padlocked. Many children were trampled to death or suffocated by the fumes. Firemen, policemen and passers-by broke windows to get to the children heaped behind the door. Injured and dying children were taken to the nearby Royal Alexandra Infirmary. It is the worst cinema disaster in British history. Safety regulations were tightened after this to ensure that cinemas had more exits, that doors opened outwards and that they were fitted with push bars. Seating capacity was also limited. I learned of this disaster when I lived near Paisley and worked with someone who had lost his brother in the tragedy. I also worked at the Royal Alexandra Infirmary in the 1970s, as a nursing auxiliary in the Coronary Care Unit.

Of course we children knew nothing of this disaster and we loved our Saturday mornings when the manager invited the children whose birthday it was on to the stage before the films and we sang 'Happy Birthday'. We also sang:

We are the boys and girls well known as
Minors of the ABC
And every Saturday all line up
To see the films we like, and shout aloud with glee.
We like to laugh and have a singsong
Such a happy crowd are we.
We're all pals together.
We're minors of the ABC.

The words were shown on the screen and a little ball bounced along above the words in time to the music. Then the programme started with cartoons like *Bugs Bunny, Daffy Duck, Woody Woodpecker, Mickey Mouse* and *Tom and Jerry*. Donald Duck was another favourite Disney character with his nephews Huey, Dewey and Louie. Then the serial started. I loved *Lassie* and *Lassie the Wonder Dog,* a collie dog who lived on a farm. We watched *Tarzan,* who swung from tree to tree while emitting a kind of yodelling cry. There were lots of cowboy films such as *Roy Rogers and Trigger,* and *The Lone Ranger and Tonto* (how can he be the Lone Ranger when he had Tonto with him?). *The Son of Zorro,* and the space action film *Flash Gordon* with his adversary Ming the Merciless were also regulars. And of course there were Martians. Space travel was complete science fiction and we thought Martians were little green men with huge egg-shaped heads and big protruding eyes. They spoke English, though, but in a metallic-sounding voice. It was actually quite worrying that Earth people wanted to explore space and maybe bring these Martians back with them and we would all be annihilated!

As the programmes proceeded we bounced excitedly up and down in our seats, cheering the goodies on and booing the baddies, and there was a crescendo of noise and pandemonium before eventually ending with the National Anthem which we all stood for. Then our motley crowd spewed out on to the pavement, dispersing in all directions and pretending to lasso each other, zapping each other, or shooting each other depending on which film had been shown that week.

Our family queued for the cinema in the evenings too. After buying our tickets we were shown to our seats in the darkened cinema by an usherette with a torch and she highlighted the empty seats for us. We enjoyed the music from the magnificent Compton 3 manual organ as it rose from the orchestra stalls at the front of the stage before the programme started at the Regal Cinema. With its vivid coloured flashing lights on the console and the soaring music, an organ was considered as an essential part of the entertainment. As the programme began we were shown adverts by Pearl and Dean, trailers, then the *Pathé News*, followed by the 'B' movie which was a less-advertised film shown as part of the double-bill. After that the lights came up and the ice cream girl walked down the aisle with her tray of ice cream tubs and ice lollies and a queue duly formed again. The main film which we had all been anticipating came next, often in Technicolor. War films were very popular where the Americans won the Second World War and all the British officers had plummy upper-class voices. Richard Attenborough and John Mills played in a lot of these films. One of the most popular British movies of 1955 was *The Colditz Story*, starring John Mills as the escape officer for the British prisoners of war at Colditz Castle, a supposedly secure castle in Saxony. At the end of the films the credits showed the date the film was produced. This is a copyright requirement. Roman numerals are used apparently because it is difficult to work out the date in the short space of time it is shown on the screen, so the population of stupid people can't work out quickly how old a programme is. People usually want to see new productions and that is the way programme makers con the masses. The whole performance lasted over three hours and then started again, so you could just stay in your seat and watch it all over again if you wanted.

Our school sports day was held on the Stray and we had sack races, three-legged races, relays, and egg and spoon races. Afterwards at school we were given our prizes of chocolate bars. We all enjoyed sweets, even though the school dentist said we should not eat them. My friend Eileen stole money from her mother's purse to buy sweets. I was shocked as I knew money was tight at home and I would never dream of stealing from my parents. I was not always good, though.

Woolworths had redesigned their counters and lowered them just at the right level for thieving fingers, and that's what we did. We called in at Woolworths on our way home from school and Pat, Susan and Eileen started to steal sweets. I didn't want to be left out but was terrified of being caught. Once or twice I stole a little Cadbury's Creme Egg and some loose sweets but was too scared to do so again. When it was Eileen's birthday she went into Woolworths one Saturday with her cousin Sandra and her birthday money. They stole toys, much more than she could have bought with her money. Her dad asked her where they had come from and Eileen told him that I had stolen them, even though I was not with them. He made them return the toys to the shop and I was never invited to Eileen's house again.

Eileen, Sandra and Pat belonged to the Baptist Church Brownies on Victoria Avenue and I wanted to go too, so I eventually persuaded Mum to let me go. Brownies was held in the church hall, down a path alongside the church. I was pleased that I was allowed to go. So, on Friday nights when I was about nine years old, I skipped along in my brown cotton dress with a narrow brown leather belt, yellow tie with tiepin, and brown woollen beret, and lined up with the other girls. The Baptist Church was where Granny Wardman was married, but I did not know that at the time, and nobody in the family mentioned it.

Brownies was strange to me. We had a 'Brown Owl' in charge of us who went 'Twit twoo'. Weird. We had to line up in our 'sixes' of Pixies, Fairies, Elves or Gnomes. I was a Fairy. I remember we did proficiency badges which we then sewed on the sleeves of our dresses. I continued in the Brownies, even when we moved to Bilton, but it was not so easy having to get the bus home.

Our family was supposed to move to Knaresborough, but we did not actually do so. Mr Morley owned a decorating business and flat in the centre of Knaresborough, in the market square. The manager of the shop had died and my mum was going to manage the shop and we were to live in the flat. But the manager's wife would not move out. So my dad drove my mum to Knaresborough each day in Morley's van and my mum worked in the shop and Dad still did decorating as well as helping in the shop. This impasse lasted for more than a year, and my parents were becoming tired and stressed. Uncle Tom kept advising Dad to leave Morley's and come to work at the Harrogate and General Hospital Board where he worked as a joiner. Dad eventually took his advice and went to work there as a decorator, painting the hospitals in the district, and also decorating the doctors' homes.

Mum and Dad got a mortgage and bought a brand new bungalow, one of four, on Bilton Lane opposite Bilton Cricket Club. Behind the bungalows was a cul-de-sac of new houses and this was Bilton Close. We moved in on 5 December 1956 after Dad had done the painting of the bungalow himself, getting an allowance for doing so. The bungalow cost £1,750 and I gave my mum the £11 which was in my Yorkshire Penny Bank account as I wanted to help. I also gave her back my bus fare when I walked home from St. Peter's School in good weather. Granny Wardman said I should keep the money myself as I had earned it, so I bought liquorice sticks and sherbet dips, or bubble gum on the way home. It was fun learning to blow the biggest bubbles then trying to lick the sticky pink goo off my face; and it made the half-hour walk feel much shorter.

One night after Brownies, as I reached the bus station, I realised I had lost my bus fare home. With my mum's warning about 'bad men' ringing in my ears, I set off to walk home in the dark. Partway a large ornate gate swung open in the wind. I thought it was a man jumping out at me. I shot off and ran the mile home in four minutes, not stopping until I reached the safety of my own front door. That was the end of Brownies.

By now it was discovered that my eyesight was bad and that I had an astigmatism. So after my eye test at school I now earned for myself the horrible pink National Health spectacles which I was told I had to look after very carefully.

Bilton

Our bungalow was new and interesting. We now had a lounge, not a living room. The plans showed three bedrooms, a kitchen, bathroom and a lounge, so we all called it 'the lounge' from now on. We had moved up in the world, even though we just lived on the ground floor. My bedroom was the centre one of the three. Dad decided we should have modern central heating and had two radiators put in the other bedrooms against the inside walls. The idea was that my room would receive some heat from the radiators on the other side of the wall. The kitchen had a boiler which kept that room warm, and we had a coal fire in the lounge where the chimney had to be swept each year to avoid a chimney fire. Uncle Tom made a drop-leaf Formica table fastened to the kitchen wall. We had a gas meter and an electricity meter in a cupboard in the kitchen which we fed with shillings when the oven went off or the lights went out. We often had power cuts too, well into the 1960s, and kept candles handy. Our bathroom suite was pink, no shower. Coloured suites became popular then, and matching coloured toilet paper, and it was a change from the ubiquitous white. Further changes in bathroom colours brought shades such as 'avocado' followed by 'aqua' then back to white. Now we can have any colour bathroom suite as long as it is white. I still helped with the washing up and drying the dishes using a Fairy soap bar before washing-up liquid was available.

Dad had a garden now and we still worked as a team digging and weeding. Our corner plot wrapped around three sides of the bungalow, and we were semi-detached. The front garden was full of bits of pottery when we moved in. They weren't Roman remains, though, but pieces of the builders' mugs and plates which were discarded from the workmen's hut for the site which had been in what was now our front garden. So Dad, Geoffrey and I set to work clearing the ground, while Mum oversaw and supervised from the lounge window. Eventually we had a lawn edged by borders of dahlias and roses with a standard rose in each corner. A weeping cherry tree guarded the gate and Nellie Moser clematis stood sentry at the front door, next to a wooden garden seat. Two apple trees divided the grass at the side garden from the vegetable plot, and we had a shed at the back, and a coal bunker outside the kitchen window. Dad put up shutters on the outside of the windows, as he had seen them when he was billeted in Belgium during the war and thought they made the bungalow attractive. Window boxes added to the appearance at the front and side of the bungalow, with a hanging basket near the front door.

Mrs Pawson came round from across the road at Myrtle Cottage, 151 Bilton Lane, which was next to the cricket club. She said Christine was her daughter and she looked to be about the same age as I was. She was right. Christine is one month younger than me. So our friendship started and we are still in touch even though Christine still lives in Bilton with her husband and son.

Premium Bonds went on sale for the first time in November 1956 and I received some £1 bonds for my Christmas present that year – they still have not won! The Chancellor of the Exchequer, Harold Macmillan, launched the scheme as a means to control inflation and encourage saving in the post-war era. The maximum investment at the time was £500 and the top prize was £1,000 and the first draw took place on Saturday 1 June 1957 by ERNIE. The Electronic Random Number Indicator Equipment was invented by one of the original Bletchley Park code breakers, and since 1957 there have been four generations of ERNIE. With continuous advances in technology, each one has become faster and smaller and ERNIE 4 takes only five hours to complete a draw, whereas the original machine would now take a hundred days! Even though my dad was a great supporter of Premium Bonds, I don't think he ever won anything, although he did think he had won when he asked to cash in £25 of his bonds, and when the money came my mum thought it was a win in a prize draw.

I continued at St. Peter's School and caught the number 12 bus into town from the corner of Grosvenor Road with my mum who went to work. I was in Mrs Haslock's class from September 1956 to July 1957, and finished the year fifth out of forty-three children.

Uncle Tom had a bright red two-seater Morgan which he used to take Auntie Jessie on day trips at the weekend. Around this time he sold the Morgan and bought a black Austin A30 which was a family car. We benefited from this as he drove us sometimes on a Sunday to the seaside, usually at Blackpool on the west coast or Scarborough on the east, and I sat excitedly on the back seat squashed between my mum and dad as we barrelled along.

Before setting off Tom had to start the car using the crank handle at the front, and usually had to give it a few energetic turns before the engine sprang into action. The indicator was an orange trafficator which popped out from the side of the car and there was one centre windscreen wiper on the front window. During the journey the windscreen became splattered with dead insects, which we don't see nowadays as there are not as many insects left because of the pesticides used, which impacts on birdlife too.

Tom sometimes treated us to lunch when we went to Blackpool and then slipped a half-crown piece (2/6d) in my pocket as we walked along the pavement to have an ice cream in an Italian ice cream parlour. The beach was always crowded and along the front were souvenir shops, stalls selling 'Kiss Me Quick' hats, bingo stalls and amusements, and 'The Laughing Policeman' at the Pleasure Beach. The landmark Blackpool Tower loomed over everything and we sometimes had a ride to the top. At the end of the day I usually fell asleep in the back of the car clutching my stick of Blackpool rock as we all trundled home.

*

According to Prime Minister Harold Macmillan we had 'never had it so good'. Full employment combined with an unprecedented rise in consumerism meant that millions of Britons saw their standard of living rise. The acquisition of material goods to improve one's social status was fuelled by 'keeping up with the Joneses'. Young people had more disposable income than ever before, and developed their own style instead of being a copy of their parents. The Teddy Boys sported clothes inspired by the styles worn by the dandies in the Edwardian era. They paraded the streets in their drainpipe trousers, luminous socks and drape jackets with velvet-trim collars. Bootlace ties, crepe-soled suede creeper shoes, and quiffed, Brylcreemed, slicked-back hair in a DA style completed the look. (Anyone

Pen and Ink Drawing of the School by the Art Master.

An image of Harrogate Grammar School in 1959.

my age will know what a DA is; young people should check the meaning.)

Coffee bars and clubs were crowded. The hand-jive was invented at the Cat's Whisker in Soho because there was no room to dance in the crowded basement. We watched rock 'n' roll, hand-jiving and artists performing on a new live BBC TV programme on a Saturday evening, *The Six-Five Special*, which launched on 16 February 1957. This filled the slot between 6pm and 7pm when the BBC abolished 'the toddlers' truce'. Pete Murray and Josephine Douglas were the presenters who introduced stars Petula Clark, Cleo Laine, Johnny Dankworth, Marty Wilde, Lonnie Donegan and Tommy Steele among others.

*

I enjoyed primary school and entered my last year there in September 1957 in Mr Bainbridge's class, but we had to be well behaved because Mr Bainbridge was a strict disciplinarian.

On 4 October 1957 the Soviet Union launched the first artificial Earth satellite. It transmitted signals which lasted for twenty-one days before the batteries ran out. It burned up on re-entering Earth's atmosphere after travelling 43.5 million miles and spending three months in orbit. This was the beginning of the Space Race between the super powers USSR and the USA. We now take for granted the use of our satellite navigation systems, but our parents would be utterly amazed at how technology has advanced in recent years.

That Christmas, in 1957, Queen Elizabeth II made the first televised Christmas Speech. As her grandfather before her, King George V, had broadcast the first Christmas Speech by radio in 1932, the Queen moved in to the modern era. The monarch's Christmas Speech has become an annual institution since 1932. Our family gathered round the TV set at 3pm to see and hear the Queen in 1957, but after a few years the tradition did not continue in our family.

We watched the news on TV in the evenings and were shocked to see and hear of the Munich air disaster on 6 February 1958 when British European Airways flight 609 crashed on its third attempt to take off from a slush-covered runway after stopping off to refuel on the flight from Belgrade to Manchester. On board was the young Manchester United football team, the 'Busby Babes', along with supporters and journalists, returning from a European Cup match in Belgrade. Of the forty-four on board, there were twenty-three fatalities and twenty-one survivors. The team had not been beaten for eleven matches and the crash destroyed a great generation of football talent. Manager Matt Busby rebuilt the team, and ten years later they won the European Cup in 1968.

On BBC TV in the late 1950s, Barry Bucknell had his *Do It Yourself* programme where he showed the public how to modernise their homes by covering up unfashionable original features with plywood. He was later attributed with destroying more homes than the Luftwaffe!

We watched Norman Wisdom comedy films in the 1950s and 1960s in which he played the hapless character Norman Pitkin who wore a too-tight suit and a tweed cloth cap, askew, with the peak turned up. Norman Wisdom came from absolute poverty to be among Britain's best box office successes of the day. Surprisingly he was a cult figure in Albania where he was one of the few Western actors whose films were allowed in the country by dictator Enver Hoxha. When Norman visited Albania in 2001, which coincided with the England football team, he was more popular than David Beckham. Norman did a lot of work and gave much to charity and was knighted in 2000.

Another popular British variety performer was Max Bygraves who seemed like a really nice man on TV when he sang his hit songs including 'You Need Hands' and 'Tulips From Amsterdam'. But he was just the opposite. Although he was married and had three legitimate children, he also had three illegitimate children who he said were 'the worst mistakes of my life' and did not contribute to their upbringing or have contact with them even though he was one of the highest-paid entertainers in the country. He said that 'life is like a self-service restaurant and you have to help yourself'. He bought a new Rolls-Royce every year and owned forty-three over the years. He often did not introduce his wife to visitors to his home, and they thought she was a servant.

*

One night I woke up and heard some heavy breathing and panting just outside my bedroom window. I was too scared to move at first, but then I jumped out of bed and rushed to wake up my dad. 'Dad, Dad! There's a man outside my bedroom window.' He got a torch and went out of the back door, followed by myself and Mum. He shone the light along the path, and there, just under my bedroom window, were two hedgehogs mating. They were making loud panting and grunting noises but soon scurried off under the beam of the light. I now know what mating hedgehogs sound like!

I threw the covers back on my bed at bedtime one night and found a fat green caterpillar crawling there. Geoffrey was at work so he was not the culprit. It had crawled from the windowbox which was under my window and into my bedroom and along the floor to my bed. I searched the whole room in case there were more. One morning I stood on a wasp when I got up and got stung on my foot. I kept my window closed from then on. There certainly was a lot of wildlife near our bungalow in Bilton.

Uncle Bill, Auntie Freda and cousin John had been to stay for a holiday and brought me a lovely sky blue and turquoise baby budgerigar which Bill had bred in the aviary in their back garden in Deal. I named the budgie Bunty after my weekly comic. Bunty loved to fly about in the lounge and perch on a vase on the windowsill and whistle and chatter to himself. He liked the echo. We used to leave him flying about on his own, but Geoffrey left the door open one day and Smutty, our black cat, came in and took one

Dad in the garden in 1959 at 104 Bilton Lane.
There were no plastic buckets in those days.

swipe at Bunty and that was the end of him. He was buried with almost full military honours in a cottonwool-lined tin in the garden.

I left primary school in July 1958 and said, 'Goodbye' to my friends, not realising that I would not see many of them again. My report says, 'A very good year's work which has brought its deserved reward. Well done.' I had passed my 11 Plus examination to go to Harrogate Grammar School, so after the summer break I then became a small fish in a large pond.

*

In September I wore my new chocolate-brown school gymslip, cream blouse, brown cardigan and blazer, brown beret and red and brown striped tie and caught the bus to school and mingled with the other 1000 youngsters. The instructions for the school uniform were, '*Blouse – cream not white; tunic or skirt – mid-brown, not nigger, mushroom, tan; shoes – brown, low broad heel. Avoid Louis and Cuban heels. Avoid flimsy sandals and slip-ons which are bad for growing feet and offer insufficient protection. The school meal is 1/- per day (1 shilling).*' This was in the days before 'political correctness' and nigger brown was a dark brown colour and Robertson's Golden Shred marmalade had a golliwog called Golly as their famous mascot and trademark. They sold collectable Golly badges, dolls, ceramics and games until Golly was 'retired' in 2002 and later replaced by Paddington Bear.

As we tumbled off the school bus we went into the Harrogate Grammar School impressive stone building, opened in 1933, on the corner of Otley Road with the main entrance on Arthur's Avenue. The school has the same motto as Harrogate, '*Arx Celebris Fontibus*', which translates from Latin as 'A citadel famous for its springs'. The William Potts of Leeds turret-style clock adorned the top of the building and was one of the first in the country to run by electricity. The imposing four-sided clock face, more than six feet in diameter, was atop a seventy-foot tower, and was the crowning glory of the school when it was opened.

This large school was confusing to me at first with lots of classrooms and timetables. Five minutes between classes were allowed to get from one room to another, and there was mayhem as everyone could be seen dashing about clutching bags and dropping books. The science classrooms were on the first floor and there was always a flurry of activity, but we were never supposed to run in school, especially on the science floor, where, we were told, dire accidents might happen from acid spills or explosions.

H. R. C. Carr (Herbert to us irreverents) was the Headmaster and boys and girls were segregated, not only in class but also in the playground and playing field, which was divided by a thick hawthorn hedge. This forbidden mixing of the sexes made us more intrigued, and clandestine meetings were often arranged.

I was in class 1C and made new friends and learned unfamiliar subjects such as algebra and geometry. We used logarithms, and weird formulas, which I have never found a use for my whole life. I really enjoyed learning French, though. There were seven forms in the first year and I was in the third form. We had gym and sports lessons with Miss Duckworth, who had started at the school in 1933. In July 1944 she had a bus accident, after which she could only work half-days until December 1945. Her accident was possibly due to the blackout. She jealously protected the beautiful wooden floor in the gym, and nobody was allowed to set foot on it in outdoor shoes. In winter we played hockey in the freezing cold on the outdoor playing fields, had swimming lessons at Starbeck Baths, and played tennis, rounders and netball in the summer. We did athletics too and practised long jump, high jump, hurdles and javelin. I was good at hurdles and had to demonstrate to the class how to run evenly over the hurdles and keep my head level. Luckily we never speared anyone with a javelin, but several years before, the chemistry master had been killed on the school playing fields when he was hit on the head by a cricket ball when he was umpiring a match.

Our sports lessons were all accompanied by Miss Duckworth's fervent and frequent blasts from her whistle. Each gym lesson we were supposed to run round the school from one gate to the other along the pavement, but most of us walked when we were out of view. At the end of term we played 'pirates' when the ribstalls were pulled away from the wall in the gym and we had to climb along them without being caught, like 'tigs off ground'. Miss Duckworth, who wore her grey hair tied back in a bun, was still fit and would often display her prowess by hanging upside down on the ribstalls. I don't think she would have been so keen to do this if she knew her face went purple.

A polio vaccine was invented in 1952, the same year as a major polio outbreak in Britain. We sometimes saw children walking with the aid of callipers. Poliomyelitis is a highly contagious viral infection which causes paralysis, breathing problems and sometimes death. There is no cure for polio, only immunisation, so we had our oral polio drops on a sugar cube at school. Patients were hospitalised in an 'iron lung', which was an airtight cylindrical steel drum, with their head and neck protruding. This machine took over their breathing. Harrogate hospital had an iron lung which was one of 1700 donated around the country and the Empire by the generosity of Lord Nuffield, William Morris, who was the motor manufacturer and philanthropist. Polio was widespread until the first vaccine was invented, since when it has been eradicated in most of the world. This was 'the good old days' of which people speak, when there was polio, smallpox, scarlet fever, diphtheria, mumps, measles and tuberculosis, which have mostly disappeared here now because of immunisation.

*

The funfair came annually to Harrogate Stray in August. I emptied my pocket money tin and Christine and I joined the other kids wasting our money on fairground rides. I indulged in roll-a-penny (the big old-fashioned pennies) and willed the pile of coins to drop each time I put a coin in the machine. If I won a few pennies I would resist the temptation to plough my money back in, and I walked away in the glow that I had overcome the urge to waste more cash. Don't forget that I am from Yorkshire. That is the height of my gambling, unless you count Premium Bonds where you can get your 'investment' back if you cash them in. My prize-less £1 bonds from the late 1950s must be almost worthless now after being eroded with inflation. I should frame them.

Next Christine and I had electrifying rides on the dodgems while sparks rained down on us from the ceiling, and menacing opponents endeavoured to crash into us at every opportunity. Our heads would then slam forward into the steering wheel, threatening us with a broken nose, and then bang backwards into the seat risking concussion.

We staggered next onto the waltzer, which I liked the best. We screamed as we were flung around in our seats when the demonically-leering fairground worker spun our car around, possibly incurring a whiplash injury. Standing at the side against the metal bar (not much health and safety there) I tried to look 'cool' as I bounced around with my coccyx rubbing against the bar. We rode until we felt sick and dizzy, or our money ran out, then staggered off the ride and tried to walk without falling over, as other teenagers rushed to grab our places on the ride. Penniless, feeling sick and disorientated and with a bruised head and bottom, I couldn't wait until the next year to waste more pocket money and have so much fun.

*

By now I was becoming interested in fashion, make-up, music and boys but not necessarily in that order. Bill Haley had used the word 'teenager' for the first time on a tour of the UK in 1957 and we were now banded into a demographic age group. When this little, dumpy, elderly (or so it seemed to us) figure with the absurd unlikely kiss curl emerged in Britain, the image did not match the sound. This was Bill Haley. He was not the sex symbol or idol we envisaged. Into this aching void gyrated Elvis Presley. Elvis 'the King' Presley attacked our senses with his music, clothes and leg-swivelling performances and made a huge impact on teenagers. He is one of the most celebrated and influential entertainers of the twentieth century, but at the time his energetic on-stage gyrations were regarded by the older generation as scandalous. Elvis never performed in Britain because his manager 'Colonel' Tom Parker was an illegal immigrant into the USA and would not be allowed back into the country if he left it. So he did not allow Elvis to perform abroad and Elvis's only visit to Britain was a brief stopover at Prestwick Airport in Ayrshire in March 1960 when he was returning to the US after serving in the Army in Germany. But, according to British singer Tommy Steele, Elvis made a surreptitious tour of London with him in 1958 where Tommy pointed out landmarks such as Buckingham Palace and the Houses of Parliament. There seems to be a complete lack of evidence and this visit has been disputed.

The basement of the 2i's coffee bar in Soho, London had live music on a small stage. It soon became popular because of its rock 'n' roll music and attracted the attention of talent spotters and music promoters such as Jack Good, Larry Parnes and Don Arden. Many British pop musicians were 'discovered' or performed there including Tommy Steele, Cliff Richard, Joe Brown and Adam Faith. Skiffle was new to the UK and the 2i's was where 'hip' youngsters could listen to the resident skiffle group the Vipers.

At his Sun Studio in Memphis rock 'n' roll pioneer Sam Phillips signed musicians such as Johnny Cash, Roy Orbison, Jerry Lee Lewis and Carl Perkins. Jerry Lee Lewis was a fantastic pianist and pounded out rock 'n' roll hits such as 'Whole Lotta Shakin' Goin' On' and 'Great Balls of Fire', but his career slumped when it was revealed in 1958, on a trip to Britain, that he had married a cousin who was only thirteen years old.

My favourites were the Everly Brothers whose harmonies I loved and who influenced many later groups including the Beatles, the Beach Boys, the Bee Gees, the Hollies, and Simon and Garfunkel. It is such a pity that brothers Don and Phil Everly could not harmonise their lives as they could harmonise their voices. They fell out and did not speak to each other for ten years from 1973 until they had a reunion concert at the Royal Albert Hall in London in September 1983. Phil Everly died on 3 January 2014.

The topic of conversation on the school bus on 4 February 1959 was the deaths of pop music stars Buddy Holly, Ritchie Valens and J. P. Richardson, known as 'The Big Bopper', in a plane crash on 3 February. It later became known as 'The Day the Music Died' in the song 'American Pie' by singer-songwriter Don McLean in 1971.

Buddy Holly, the unlikely-looking pop star, wearing huge black-rimmed glasses, was phenomenal. His tragically short career only lasted about eighteen months, but his music is timeless.

Musicians took long journeys on cold, uncomfortable tour buses between venues in the United States in winter, and were affected by flu and even frostbite. Buddy Holly decided to charter a plane from Clear Lake to Moorhead, Minnesota for some of the group playing on the 'Winter Dance Party' tour of the Midwest. Piloted by twenty-one-year-old Roger Peterson the light aircraft took off late at night in snowy conditions with poor visibility and crashed soon after take-off. It emerged that the young pilot was not qualified to operate in weather which required flying solely by instruments. Any instrument training that Peterson had received was in airplanes with a different attitude gyroscope which displayed the aircraft pitch attitude information in exactly the opposite way from the Beechcraft Bonanza he was flying that night. So with low clouds obscuring the stars and no visible horizon or ground lights he would have thought that the plane was climbing when in fact it was descending. It nose-dived and crashed into a cornfield at about 170 miles per hour, killing all four on board.

I listened to pop music played by Radio Luxembourg on my transistor radio in bed at night. The reception was poor and kids at school said you

Mum and me on our Torquay summer holiday in 1959.

could hear better if you put the radio on an upturned metal saucepan, so that's what I did. I usually fell asleep and woke up in the middle of the night to the crackling of the radio.

I finished the school year eighth out of thirty-one in the class and started the summer break. Mum, Dad and I went for a week's holiday on the train to Torquay. I was amazed at the red stone and soil near Torquay as we rode on the train along the south coast. Geoffrey was twenty-one by then so he was not interested in coming with us. He made a good choice. It was not a very successful week. We stayed in an apartment and the dog next door barked most nights and we didn't get much sleep. We caught a bus one day to Goodrington Sands, because we had heard the sand there was beautiful and white. As soon as we had ensconced ourselves on the beach, it started to rain, so back to the bus it was. The only trouble was that they were open-top buses and the ones which passed us were all full on the bottom deck, and the drivers were not allowed to take passengers on the open deck in bad weather. So we stood for an hour in the relentless pouring rain until one bus driver took pity on us and stopped. Our little family managed to squeeze as standing passengers on the bottom deck, and the others braved the weather upstairs, but we were all drenched.

Christine and I had begun to go to the cricket club in summer and helped with making the teas on a Saturday afternoon, buttering loaves of bread for the sandwiches. The cakes came from the Avenue Bakery on trays and the teapots were filled from a big urn of boiling water. (The Avenue Bakery has appeared in two episodes of the TV programme *Heartbeat*.) Bilton Cricket Club teas were always popular and are still renowned in the Airedale and Wharfedale League. In that year the cricket club obtained the deeds for the ground on Bilton Lane and a commemorative cine film was made. One Sunday morning the driver of the Bilton number 20 red Routemaster bus was asked if he would co-operate by letting a few players and spectators board the bus and then be filmed disembarking as if we were going to a cricket match. So that is why Christine and I, age twelve and walking hand-in-hand in our summer dresses, sandals and little white ankle socks, are in the film which we now have as a DVD, thanks to Christine and her husband Ian. The film shows fields where there is now a housing estate, and the steam train puffing along in the distance.

*

Bilton was first recorded in the Domesday Book in 1086 and was historically in the parish of Knaresborough, and part of Knaresborough Forest. There were many old farms in the Bilton area until just after the middle of the twentieth century when the farms and farmland were taken over by housing developments. Christine and I used to go for fresh eggs down Bilton Lane to Bilton Grove Farm where the Barrett family lived then. We crossed the poultry yard to the farm door and stood and waited for our eggs. The meat hooks still hung from the ceiling inside. The farm was demolished in the mid-1960s for the development of the Meadowcroft housing estate and it was said that the rats all escaped to nearby houses. My first home after I was married in October 1967 was a bungalow in Meadowcroft built by Wrightson and Robinson. Of course the bungalow wasn't ready to move into as promised when we were married so Dad helped us with the painting during the cold winter months. We did as he had done with his bungalow and got an allowance for painting it ourselves. We cleaned all the rubble out from under the floorboards as well.

Beyond Bilton Grove Farm was the railway which was opened through Bilton in 1848. Trainspotting was a national pastime for most boys in the

Mum, me and Christine on a day out at Scarborough,
still in our white ankle socks.

1950s and 1960s and the level crossing at Bilton was no exception. A lot of boys were enthusiastic about trains and railways and many wanted to be train drivers. So boys gathered at stations and crossings wearing their knee-length grey shorts and knee-high socks, shirt, V-necked pullover and peaked cap and clutching their ABC books of locomotives by Ian Allan, a railway enthusiast who worked as a clerk at Waterloo Station on Southern Railways. He produced a booklet containing a numerical list of loco numbers and details of their classes and placed a small classified ad in the *Railway World* magazine offering the booklet for one shilling. All 2000 copies were quickly sold and a reprint ordered with a new title, *ABC of Southern Locomotives*, followed by *The Great Western*, *LMS* (London, Midland and Scottish Railway) and *LNER* (London and North Eastern Railway), and a book on London Transport of which all 20,000 copies were sold in days. Trainspotting was born and boys looked out for steam engines such as *The Mallard*, *Sir Nigel Gresley*, *The Flying Scotsman*, *Dominion of Canada* and *The Bittern*.

There used to be a narrow gauge railway which opened in 1908 south of the main line in Bilton. This was used to enable coal to be unloaded from railway wagons in the sidings into road wagons which were hauled by steam locomotives to the gas works at New Park. This was known as 'The Barber Line' after Mr F. Barber who was the company chairman of Harrogate Gas Company at the time. The railway closed in 1956 and was dismantled immediately.

Beyond the rail line the road dips down to a row of alms houses and the Gardeners Arms, and the temperature also drops noticeably and Christine and I thought the buildings must be haunted. The Gardeners Arms, also mentioned in the Domesday Book, is a traditional old pub with stone flags, stone fireplaces and small rooms like the 'piggery' and 'wrinklies bar'. There is a garden with the river at the bottom. Of course we did not frequent the place in those days because we were too young. I remember there was a storm about 1969 when the whole of the Harrogate area was battered by hailstones the size of golf balls which knocked birds out of trees. A huge black cloud passed over and it became as dark as night. Windows were broken – apparently every pane in greenhouses in Killinghall – and roads flooded, and the garden wall in the dip at the Gardeners Arms was demolished by the floods.

Further along the road is Bilton Hall, possibly the most historically important building in the Harrogate area. In 1380 John of Gaunt, Lord of Knaresborough and son of Edward III, ordered a new hunting lodge to be built in the deer park of Bilton Park. This building evolved and became Bilton Hall and was owned in the middle of the sixteenth century by the powerful Slingsby family. (It was William Slingsby who discovered the curative Harrogate waters.) The Crown held Bilton Park until it was sold by Charles I in 1628. Over the years Bilton Hall changed hands several times and is now a retirement home.

The rag and bone man still rode down Bilton Lane on his horse and cart. The 'pop' man called and we bought bottles of dandelion and burdock, ginger beer or ice cream soda. We also bought our pop from Gibson's shop on King Edward's Drive and received a few pennies back when we returned the empty bottles for recycling. Our bags of coal were delivered in the coal wagon. Days passed in an orderly fashion. Dad went to work on his 125cc motorbike with his sandwich lunch fastened safely in his bag crossed over his chest. Mum and I went on the bus each morning, she to work and me to school with my homework in my satchel. My school reports said that I worked hard, was a steady worker and was making good progress. I was enjoying English and French and Art lessons. Geoffrey went to work in Bradford on his motorbike and came home on days off and at weekends. Life was solid like the bricks in the walls. It ticked on like a well-oiled clock, day after day, until one day it stopped.

Being Thirteen

Thirteen is an unlucky number. Nothing awful happened when I was thirteen, not until a month before my fourteenth birthday.

One day I caught a bad cold with a temperature. I often caught colds but this one concerned my parents, so Mum walked to the phone box up the road to phone the doctor. Not many people had phones at home in those days, or cars either for that matter. I was dispatched off to bed – Mum and Dad's bed of course – in the best bedroom, to await the doctor. The doctor had to be shown into the best bedroom.

He arrived with his black bag and friendly face and put me at my ease. 'Let's see what's wrong with you, young lady, shall we?' He brought a stethoscope and thermometer out of his bag, like rabbits out of a hat. 'You have tracheaitis and a temperature of 104,' he declared after examining me and sounding my chest. 'Now you stay in bed and keep warm and I'll see you in a few days' time.' Not just a cold but trachaeitis, and a temperature to boot.

I was sent back to my own bed but couldn't sleep and thrashed about, hot and restless. Eventually Mum said, 'You'd better have a hot bath and I'll change your bedding.' Feeling weak but glowing from the hot water I prepared to slip into bed again. Oh lovely, Mum had put the electric blanket on. I unplugged it and snuggling down and curling up like a foetus I was warm and cosy in my womb-like cocoon and drifted off into a welcome untroubled sleep. I awoke a while later drenched in sweat and Mum decided that I had sweated out the fever. I felt much better.

That night we were all in our beds fast asleep when there was a loud, hard knocking like a policeman's knock on the front door at about 1.15am which woke us all up. Nobody hammered on our front door in the middle of the night. Dad went to answer the door in his pyjamas while Mum and I hovered in the hallway behind him, blinking and peering at the front door. He cautiously opened the door and the hall light shone on a pale face above a dark uniform. It *was* a policeman. He said, 'Good evening, sir. I am sorry to trouble you, but does someone in the house own a motorbike with the registration number...' and he looked at his notebook and read out the number plate.

Dad said, 'Yes, it's my son's motorbike.'

'There's been a bad road accident. All road accidents are classed as bad so don't worry too much. He's in Chapel Allerton Hospital in Leeds. The police in Leeds informed us. I am from the Harrogate police force.'

Dad told him, 'Geoffrey must have been going back to his "digs" in Bradford. He works in Bradford during the week and comes home at the weekends.'

The policeman asked for the address. I knew I had the address in my dressing table drawer in my bedroom so I went to get it. I remember quite clearly having a sense of panic as I opened the drawer and thought, 'What if he dies?' I shook my head to clear it of the uninvited thoughts and realised with relief that that sort of thing happens to other people. Of course it doesn't always happen to other people, and it happened to us that night.

'Have you got a car, sir?' asked the policeman.

'No, but my brother Tom has. It's not too far away, at 76 St. John's Road.'

'Well, if you'd like to get dressed I'll take you up there.'

So Dad got dressed, Mum flustered and I hoped. It was decided that Uncle Tom could take my mum and dad to the hospital and Auntie Jessie would stay with me. I was rather apprehensive as Auntie Jessie was a bit strange and I was not looking forward to her spending the night with me. In fact she was very nice and kind and spent some time sitting on the end of my bed chatting to me and trying to reassure me, but apprehension hung over us like a storm cloud that night.

I could not sleep and spent the rest of the long night wide awake in bed, while Auntie Jessie sat and waited in the lounge. As dawn was beginning to lighten the sky my mum, dad and Uncle Tom arrived home. Jessie went to open the door while I was still in bed. Mum said, 'He's gone. Don't tell Christine.' Oh no!! I burst into tears and arms wrapped around me. I don't think my parents knew what to say as they were in so much pain and shock themselves.

*

Arriving at the hospital through the cold, dark night, saying little and thinking a lot, they found the doctor was waiting for them at the door with an anguished look on his face. 'I am very sorry to tell you that your son has just died.' They knew. 'He was in the operating theatre, and we were going to amputate his leg, but he was too badly injured. I am so sorry. I have a motorbike myself but I'm going to sell it now.'

That night changed all our lives.

We sat most of the next day in a tight little knot in the lounge and Granny Wardman came, and some of the neighbours came when they found out the news, and the vicar came. We couldn't conjure Geoffrey back, couldn't cheat Fate by rewinding the clock a few seconds and changing History, no matter how much we wanted to. Dad wandered about his beloved garden staring at his dahlias for a while. Nothing had changed in the garden. Life was going on. The next-door neighbour was surprised to see him. He said that he had heard that my dad had died on his motorbike in a road accident, and Dad explained that it was Geoffrey and not him. He probably wished it had been him. Nobody should have to bury a child.

Geoffrey had come to Harrogate on the Tuesday evening after work to get a special light or a part for his motorbike from his friend who worked in a motorbike shop. The part was not there on the Saturday when Geoffrey was home for the weekend and he was eager to collect it and fix it to his 1000cc Triumph motorbike so he had come to Harrogate on the Tuesday evening. After seeing his friend he must have decided to go back to Bradford instead of coming home, as he did not have his house keys in his belongings which the hospital staff gave to Mum and Dad afterwards. There were his bloodied clothes and blood-covered leather motorcycle gloves, some small change, and not much else. They said they had to return the belongings to the next of kin, but I thought it was extremely insensitive to return the blood-soaked clothes in which their son had died.

I sat on the bed in his bedroom and cried to myself over those bloodstained motorcycle gloves, which were not damaged in any other way. The strap of his motorcycle helmet had seemingly been cut in the accident, which happened at Pool Bank. A car with a couple of Scotsmen on holiday had crashed into Geoffrey and dragged him and his motorbike along the road. Dad went to the scene the next day on his own motorbike to see if he could make sense out of it all and to maybe come to some understanding of what had happened, or maybe he just had to see exactly where the accident had occurred. There he found one of Geoffrey's shoes way along the road in the direction the Scotsmen were travelling which proves that they had collided with him and dragged him along the road. They must have been travelling fast by the distance that Dad found Geoffrey's shoe.

It was a twenty-year-old who was driving, with his brother in his thirties. This was before the breathalyser tests came in, and there were no witnesses and no other traffic nearby. The people in the pub on the corner heard the impact and came out to see, but nobody actually saw the accident. Someone must have jumped the traffic lights and, of course, we did not think it was Geoffrey. He had never had an accident, had never even come off his bike as far as we knew, and he loved his motorbike. Dad said that when he himself was young he was always coming off his motorbike, but to Geoffrey his bike was a machine to look after, take pride in and keep in good working order. He was an engineer, after all.

The next horrible event was that Dad had to go and identify his body which must have been dreadfully difficult. I think he could only bring himself to glance at him, but said he saw his bruised face and recognised his nose. Tom had driven him there. It must have been terrible for him too as Geoffrey was like a son to him because he and Jessie had no children of their own. Geoffrey and Tom worked together on a Sunday in Tom's shed workshop in the garden.

A policeman came to the house to ask Dad some questions the next day and they talked in the kitchen while Mum and I were in the lounge. Dad mentioned Geoffrey's belongings in answer to a question and the policeman was surprised. He had not even been told that Geoffrey had died.

A reporter from the Harrogate newspaper came round too for information to write a report for the newspaper. The accident had happened late on Tuesday evening 20 September and Geoffrey died in the early hours of Wednesday 21 September, Dad's birthday. Maybe Geoffrey had intended coming home as a surprise on the Tuesday evening mid-week but had forgotten to bring our house key with him. He might have thought it was a bit too late and Mum and Dad just may have gone to bed and he did not want to disturb them or worry us. I will never know.

The funeral was arranged for the following Saturday which was 24 September, and happened to be Granny Hodgson's birthday. Probably that was the earliest and most convenient time for people to come to the funeral without having to arrange time off work. Funerals took place quickly in those days and also it was not easy getting time off work without losing pay.

Four of Geoffrey's friends from Harrogate and workmates from the English Electric Company in Bradford were to be pallbearers. His workmates made a collection and afterwards Mum and Dad used the money towards a headstone for the grave. They bought a plot for three people for Geoffrey and themselves in Stonefall cemetery. I felt upset as they had not included provision for me in the grave as well but, rightly so, they explained that I would grow up and get married and would not need a plot with them as I would probably be buried with my own husband and family. Nevertheless I did feel excluded at this vulnerable time.

Mum did not have a black coat so they went into town and she bought a black and white small-herringbone-patterned wool coat. I was not allowed to go to the funeral as they said it would be too distressing for me, and I was still not too well. I went to Christine's house and stayed there with her and Joe and Gladys, her parents, until my family came back home.

Mum said that the chapel was full of people but she was too upset to see who they all were. In the days that followed the postman brought lots of sympathy letters and cards. I remember one of them said, 'It is better to have loved and lost than never to have loved at all', and another, 'Whom the Gods love die young.'

The inquest was held on 13 October. The car driver tried to make out that Geoffrey had gone into them until Dad had the courage to stand up and say he had found Geoffrey's shoe along the road in the direction they were travelling. He was not used to courtrooms. There did not seem to have been much of a police investigation. It was just the death of another young motorcyclist.

Extract from *The Yorkshire Post*, Wednesday 21 September 1960, page 12:

Motor Cyclist Hurt

Early today Geoffrey Wardman, Bilton Lane, Harrogate, was seriously injured when the motor cycle he was driving at Horsforth was involved in a collision. He was taken to St. James's Hospital, Leeds, and then transferred to the neuro-surgical unit at Chapel Allerton Hospital where he was stated to be "seriously ill."

Extract from *The Yorkshire Evening Post*, Wednesday 21 September 1960, page 8:

Bramhope Fatality

A Harrogate motor-cyclist, Geoffrey Howard Wardman, Bilton Lane, has died in Chapel-Allerton Hospital, Leeds following an accident between his motor-cycle and a car at the Dyneley crossroads at Bramhope. The driver of the car, Gilbert McKie, Ballaird, Wigtown, Scotland, and his passenger, Thomas McKie, are in hospital.

Of course the whole experience for our family was very harrowing. I could not sleep in my own bedroom without waking up from dreaming of Geoffrey lying injured in the road and covered in blood. I was so upset and frightened that Dad dismantled my bed and squeezed it into their bedroom doorway so that I could be nearer to them at night for a couple of weeks.

Granny Wardman came round for a Saturday evening or Sunday lunch as usual and came down our path upset and crying because Geoffrey would not be there. She was usually such a strong woman but she was about eighty years old and it took its toll on her. She had already lost a husband and daughter in the 1930s in very sad circumstances, within a few months of each other and both at young ages.

I would lay the table at mealtimes for the four of us, momentarily forgetting that he would not be there. I used to come in from school and sit in the kitchen doing my homework and think that maybe it was not Geoffrey who had been in the accident but a friend to whom he had lent his bike; or that something else had happened to him and he had wandered off and lost his memory and that he would come home soon. Anything to stop thinking that he would never come in the door again. What would I do if he did come in the door? I had lost my big brother, my hero.

Dad never again celebrated his birthday. A few years later, after several tests, Mum was diagnosed with multiple sclerosis which the doctor said was possibly caused by the shock of Geoffrey's death. I had no other brothers or sisters. I would never have a sister-in-law nor any nephews and nieces. Our branch of the Wardman name died with Geoffrey. He was only twenty-two years old. Geoffrey died that night and was gone for always, only existing in our memories. It is such a long time ago but, as you see, I remember that time so vividly, as I am sure anyone who has lost a loved one in tragic circumstances would be the same. The year Geoffrey died was 1960. I am a pensioner myself now, married, and also a grandma. I am very lucky, and proud of my family.

Thirteen is an unlucky number. Nothing awful happened when I was thirteen, not until a month before my fourteenth birthday when my brother was killed in a road accident. It was the night which changed all our lives.

The Swinging Sixties

The clock was eventually wound up again and the ticking started, but not as strongly nor as evenly, but our lives went on. Mum did not tell my school that Geoffrey had died and I tried to carry on as usual, as we all did. My position in the form dropped back. At Christmas Uncle Tom bought me a Grundig record player and Christine and I used our pocket money to buy records in town and we listened entranced in her front room or in our lounge. We could stack ten 45rpm vinyl singles records on the turntable, but soon gave that up because the records wobbled so much as they went round. Favourites of mine were Billy Fury, Marty Wilde, Roy Orbison and Ricky Nelson, as well as the Everly Brothers of course. Christine liked Adam Faith best.

In a study commissioned for the TV programme *The Sixties* for Yesterday TV channel, the 'Swinging Sixties' has been named as the most defining decade of the twentieth century in British history, famed for its iconic fashion, significant events and groundbreaking music.

Fender, the American manufacturer of stringed instruments and amplifiers, mass-produced the Stratocaster electric guitar in 1954. The electric guitar was the perfect instrument for rock 'n' roll. The first Fender Stratocaster in Britain was Hank Marvin's fiesta red Strat with gold-plated fittings which made an appearance in 1959. Cliff Richard and the Shadows had great success in pop music in the late 1950s and early 1960s. Hank Marvin, the lead guitarist in the Shadows, was impressed by Buddy Holly's Fender Stratocaster guitar so Cliff ordered one and now Hank Marvin is associated with his red Stratocaster, and bought several other Stratocasters over the years. I went on a week's summer holiday (plug for Cliff Richard!) to Blackpool with Christine and her mum and dad in the early 1960s, and Christine and her mum and myself got tickets to a summer season show one evening to see Cliff and the Shadows. We sat in the balcony but Christine and I were not sitting for long. We were jumping up and down with everyone else – except Christine's mum, who said the balcony was bouncing all over the place and she thought it was going to collapse.

There was a plethora of musical genres and artists emerging in the late 1950s and 1960s both in the USA and Britain. From the early days of blues, country and gospel music in the States came rock 'n' roll (reputedly a term that black people used for sexual intercourse!), folk and protest artists such as Pete Seeger, Joan Baez and Bob Dylan. There were vocal groups, rock groups, bands, duos, solo artists singing and playing ballads, rock, comedy records and skiffle. Even South African singer Miriam Makeba had a hit with 'The Click Song'. Frank Ifield's falsetto and yodelling songs were hits too. He was the first UK-based artist to reach No. 1 three times in the UK in succession. Lonnie Donegan was the 'King of Skiffle', which was played on a washboard, tea-chest base and guitar or banjo. There is not the variety of music nowadays as there was then, and sixties music is still popular with its own radio programmes. The Shadows developed the 'walk' from watching black American band the Treniers at the 1958 Jerry Lee Lewis tour of the UK. Hank Marvin and Bruce Welsh were impressed by the way the saxophone players moved in unison in tempo with the music, and they developed their own sequence. We listened to what Jerry Lee Lewis called 'all the Bobbies' – Bobby Vee, Bobby Rydell, Bobby Vinton and Bobby Darin. There were many female singers too such as Americans Brenda Lee and Connie Francis, and the UK's Petula Clark, Alma Cogan, Shirley Bassey and Helen Shapiro. But I preferred the male vocalists.

At school my progress was mixed. I enjoyed English, French, Biology and Art lessons. A great teacher, highly powdered and perfumed Miss Agatha Johnson took us for English and I still remember some of the things she said: 'Swearing shows a lack of vocabulary' and 'A person is hanged and a picture is hung.' She wore upswept wing spectacles, rather like Dame Edna Everage, while she presided over our lessons. Herbert Christie took us for Art and kids suggested that if Agatha Johnson married Herbert Christie then she would be Agatha Christie, a very unlikely scenario we decided as we watched him mince along the corridor.

Me in a shirtwaister dress with a wide belt.

Another great teacher was Miss Sharples who taught us French. She was the Deputy Headmistress from September 1959 and wore tweed skirts and sensible shoes. Some of my other school results reflected the quality of teaching, in my opinion. We had 'Dozy' Joe Green for Chemistry and the boys would connect the Bunsen burner to the water tap, when his back was turned, and a spout of water shot up to the ceiling. Another teacher was 'Flogger' Cogger. Actually he did not flog us but the name rhymed. Caning still happened, though, in those days and pupils were sometimes sent to the Headmaster for the cane.

We had a new lady teacher for Maths and the boys learned that if they messed about, then the whole class had to stand for the rest of the lesson. Obviously she played into their hands and we often scraped back our chairs and stood shuffling from one foot to the other until the bell rang, and therefore did not learn much. She did not stay long.

'Snotty' Sutcliffe was another of our teachers. If we looked up after completing a question in a test, we caught him picking his nose and eating it!

Music was taught in the main hall, which has a beautiful parquet floor, by Mr Webber who often threw a blackboard rubber at some recalcitrant, inattentive pupil. Most male teachers wore gowns and Mr Webber was one of them. He strode along the corridors like a ship in full sail with his black gown flowing behind him.

'Juicy' Lucy Davidson took us for Geography, and William 'Billy' Bundred took us for History. Certain historical events happened on different dates. For instance, sometimes the Battle of Hastings occurred in 1066 but in another lesson it happened in 1067 or 1068, depending on what date came into Mr Bundred's mind, so when I looked back at my notes I was understandably confused.

By then we were sensibly in mixed classes and Ernest 'Ernie' Gordon Hill was Headmaster. In Biology, our young male teacher, Mr Melton, dissected a rabbit. We gathered round and peered as he sliced the poor unfortunate creature – already dead of course. Then he stretched the legs out and pinned the paws to the corners of the table. We heard a strangled cry from behind, and turned round to see the biggest lad in the class in a crumpled heap on the floor.

Limited sex education was given to our bunch of adolescents by this same young, embarrassed male biology teacher. He described the reproductive system in rabbits, and then muttered that the system was similar in human beings. Our burgeoning interest in sex was fuelled by the publication of D. H. Lawrence's *Lady Chatterley's Lover* published by Penguin Books. Legal proceedings had been taken in the UK at the Old Bailey against Penguin Books under the Obscene Publications Act 1959. The watershed six-day trial lasted from 20 October to 2 November 1960. In his lengthy closing statement, Gerald Gardiner, counsel for the defence, stated that the book must be judged as a whole and not for particular passages. The jury found in favour of Penguin Books who quickly sold three million copies of the book, one of which landed in our hands at school. The book, with the interesting passages highlighted by someone, was passed around and read enthusiastically and giggled over. It ended up well-thumbed and dog-eared. Similarly we acquired copies of *A Kind of Loving* by Stan Barstow, *Peyton Place* by Grace Metalious, and *Saturday Night and Sunday Morning*. Our sex education was complete.

*

1961 saw the introduction of the oral contraceptive pill available on the National Health Service in Britain. I think it was possibly the greatest scientific invention of the twentieth century. It gave women control over their sex lives and how many children they wanted, but at the time, it was not realised how revolutionary this was. The medical establishment was not ready to make the pill freely available, and it was mainly prescribed to older married women who already had children and who did not want any more. The government did not want to be seen to be promoting promiscuity or 'free love'. Previously women had to rely on men for contraception but now women had control. The implied promise in a relationship was that if a woman became pregnant, then the man would marry her. In 1950s Britain there were still Victorian attitudes towards sex. There was a stigma attached to unmarried mothers who often were sent away to have their babies who were then taken away for adoption. As a consequence of this tiny pill there were less unwanted children available for adoption, but also children were more valued than previously. All I can say is that 'free love' did not reach Harrogate and couples who cohabited and were not married were still regarded as 'living in sin'.

When the pill was first introduced it was regarded as completely safe and very effective, and became highly successful. Now the side effects are known to include mood swings, depression, headaches, nausea and weight gain.

Another 'wonder drug' which was used in Britain from April 1958 until late 1961 was Distaval, or thalidomide. It was prescribed by doctors for the short-term treatment of morning sickness in pregnant women, typically in the first three months of their pregnancy, exactly when the baby is forming. At this time the use of medications during pregnancy was not strictly controlled, and drugs were not thoroughly tested for potential harm to the foetus. It was eventually noticed that babies with devastating birth malformations were being born in several countries. The Australian obstetrician William McBride and the German paediatrician Widukind Lenz suspected a link between birth defects and the drug. William McBride published a letter in *The Lancet* making this connection public knowledge and Chemie Grünenthal, the German pharmaceutical company which developed the drug, reluctantly withdrew it in November 1961.

Many babies who were affected by thalidomide were miscarried, still born or died soon after birth. It has been estimated that 24,000 babies were

Christine with me and a monkey, which was thrust into my arms
by the seaside photographer.

born worldwide of which 2000 were born in the UK. The main impairments caused by thalidomide affect the limbs, often misshapen, shortened, or entirely limbless with hands and feet, again often malformed, which arise almost from the trunk. Thalidomide also affected the eyes and ears and internal organs.

In February 1968 Distillers Ltd, the company which marketed Distaval in the UK, paid damages to sixty-two thalidomide-impaired children born in the UK. This was widely recognised as inadequate and, following a high-profile campaign, a final settlement of £20 million was agreed in 1973. The Thalidomide Trust was established to provide support and assistance to thalidomide survivors, many of whom are alive today. In 2017 the BBC *Call the Midwife* series featured a number of stories regarding thalidomide in their programmes about midwifery in 1950s and 1960s London.

*

On Saturday mornings Christine and I usually went into town on the red double-decker bus to do some shopping for my mum, and for Granny

Hodgson too. The driver sat in splendid isolation in his cab, and the conductor or conductress (clippie) issued the tickets from the machine hanging round his or her neck. The upstairs lingered with stale smoke, and the ceiling, which used to be cream, was nicotine-stained brown. We clambered up the stairs at the back of the bus and rushed to sit in the front seats to get an elevated view of our surroundings. All the kids rushed to get an upstairs front seat. I have been up Blackpool Tower, the Eiffel Tower, Seattle Space Needle, the CN Tower in Toronto, the Empire State Building in New York and the Burj Khalifa in Dubai, so the view from the top deck of a bus is not as interesting to me now as it once was. I usually sit downstairs nowadays, but it is fun to go upstairs with my granddaughter and try and get the front seats again. It is even better now that I can use my senior citizen bus pass and get a free ride. Yippee!

In town we went to the Co-op to see Christine's dad, Joe. He was often slicing bacon, then wrapping it in cellophane before ironing it to seal the wrapper. I did not realise until then how the packets were sealed.

At home we had fish and chips for Saturday dinner (or do I say lunch?) from the fish shop on King Edward's Drive, and in the afternoon Dad and I sometimes worked as a team making chicken soup. He peeled potatoes, celery, carrots and onions then I diced them to go in a large pot with a boiling fowl which simmered on the gas hob during the afternoon. On Sundays we usually had roast beef, which was tender in those days, even with my mum's cooking! Accompanying our roast beef we had Yorkshire puddings, of course, and Sunday potatoes. That was the name I gave roast potatoes because that was the only day of the week we had them. Chicken and turkey were for Christmas. We followed the roast dinner with rice pudding which Mum made 'while the oven was on'. Dad and I had shandy on Sunday with our meal as a treat and shared a bottle of beer in a glass with lemonade on top. I liked ginger beer shandy best. Dad never went to the pub, neither did Christine's dad. The families I knew spent their money on their homes and families and did not usually gamble, smoke or drink, except of course there was a bottle of sherry and Lamb's Navy Rum at Christmas in our home.

*

I started back at school in the autumn term of 1961 in Form 4B1, still in the third form of seven. I had chosen my options for the GCE (General Certificate of Education) 'O' level examinations and chose History instead of Geography. I also chose German because I enjoyed and did well in French. Unfortunately I had these classes with the two A forms above me and I felt that I was being left behind.

Dr Eric 'Chips' Fisher taught us History. He did not really teach us but talked to us right through the lesson and we had to take notes. He glared at students and there was no misbehaving in class. He was a very formidable character and did not inspire me. He had been teaching at the grammar school since 1928 and did not instil any enthusiasm in me. I did not enjoy Geography or History at school but now I find the subjects interesting.

Our top three forms were taught German by Dr Mayer who had joined the school in 1946 after fleeing Nazi persecution in Vienna. A favourite request from some students to divert his attention from learning the language was, 'Please, sir, tell us again how you escaped from the Nazis in Austria.' I cannot remember much about our German classes except he used to shout at us, 'Vot is ze matter viz you? Vy can't you understand it?' So I did not do well in German, which is a pity because I really enjoyed French.

We had the opportunity to go on a French exchange visit, but my mum would not allow me to go as she was working and could not reciprocate the hospitality to a French student. I did persuade my mum, though, to let me have my dinner money and to stop having the unappetising school meals. So my friends and I brought sandwiches from home or went down Cold Bath Road to buy fish and chips. Shirley had some black Sobranie Russian cigarettes and we practised smoking on a seat in a shelter in the Valley Gardens. We felt very sophisticated trying these slim black cigarettes with a gold tip. We smoked in the school toilets too or shared our money and bought a packet of five ciggies and smoked them in the cinema on holidays. You could smoke in the cinema then of course. Thankfully I could not get used to the smoke going up my nose and in my eyes so I did not persevere or by now my lungs would be shot, my teeth rotten and my skin all wrinkled.

We sometimes walked to the tuck shop on Otley Road and bought crisps and bread rolls to make crisp sandwiches, but if we were caught by a prefect without our school berets we got a detention. The same went for wearing our berets on the school bus. It is a good job we were not caught smoking.

Girls now wore tights instead of stockings and we rolled our skirts over at the waistband to shorten them. My granddaughter does the same now. We wore shirtwaister dresses too with layers of net petticoat underneath and cinched at the waist with a wide elastic belt. I sat in a hot bath with my jeans on to shrink them, as recommended by friends, but it didn't really work. We can buy skinny jeans now and even super skinny!

One evening, after a school play, I missed my curfew. At the ungodly hour of 10.15pm Dad put his trousers on over his pyjamas and was sent out to search for me. He located me strutting home in my stiletto heels and pencil skirt, in the otherwise silent streets. I managed to hitch the said skirt to an unseemly height and hop on the pillion seat of his motorbike. We proceeded home along the dark and deserted streets. The hard-working residents of Bilton retired early to prepare for the challenges of their working day.

*

In January 1962 there was an outbreak of smallpox in Bradford which was traced to a nine-year-old girl who had travelled with her family from Pakistan in December 1961. It was at first thought that she had malaria but her condition worsened and she died at the end of December in the Children's Hospital in Bradford without the real disease being identified. The unvaccinated pathologist, Dr Norman Ainsley, who performed her postmortem also died from smallpox. In all, five Bradford hospitals were implicated in the outbreak and these were closed with no admissions, discharges or visitors. Vaccination centres were set up, contacts traced and the outbreak was contained, but six people died. Unfortunately the smallpox vaccination can have some unpleasant and serious side effects and my dad, who worked at hospitals and doctors' homes in the Harrogate area, had to have the vaccination. His upper left arm became very sore, swollen, painful and inflamed, and I remember it because he was always so uncomplaining and I know how uncomfortable he was. There was also an outbreak in Wales at about the same time, again caused by someone travelling from Pakistan. Nineteen people died before the outbreak was over. Smallpox is an acute, highly contagious disease caused by variola virus and it killed several European monarchs including Queen Mary II of England and Louis XV of France. There is no effective treatment and about 30% of those infected die. The survivors are left with deeply pockmarked faces. Through vaccination smallpox has been eradicated and now only stocks of live smallpox remain in laboratories.

The communications satellite Telstar was launched in July 1962 and successfully relayed the first television pictures, telephone calls and fax images through space. This was another fantastic achievement and was celebrated by the English band the Tornados who had a number one hit in both the USA and UK in 1962 with their electronic-sounding instrumental 'Telstar'.

1962 brought *Dr No*, the first of the cult James Bond film series, created by novelist Ian Fleming in 1953. Spy-master Ian Fleming was the son of Valentine Fleming, who was MP for Henley-on-Thames until he was killed in the First World War. Sean Connery was the first fictional 007 James Bond actor and played the character in six films. I prefer Roger Moore (erstwhile knitwear model) in the role as I think he plays James Bond with sophistication and a sarcastic tongue-in-cheek style, but I know more people prefer Sean Connery.

*

Christine and I continued to go to the cricket club in summer and progressed to scoring at the matches. The cricket club was a good place to meet boys! I got some exercise by signalling 'four', 'bye' and 'leg bye' from the scoreboard to the umpire and Christine exercised by rolling the numbers round on the board to show the scores. I went on the bus too with the first team on their away matches in the Airedale and Wharfedale League on Saturdays to grounds at Silsden, Addingham, Menston, Burley, Horsforth, Steeton, Otley, Ilkley, Gargrave, Skipton and Guiseley, the home of Harry Ramsden's famous fish and chips, and of course we had to try some.

After uncharacteristically over-imbibing while celebrating after a match, one of the players, David Broadley, earned the nickname 'Bloodshot' Broadley. A group of us went one night to see the Everly Brothers perform in Leeds, but actually it was only Phil Everly who appeared on stage as Don was reported to have had a nervous breakdown. Christine and I sang out at the tops of our voices and I wouldn't go home until I had seen Phil at the stage door. So Christine, Pete, Roy and I waited, but I think he had left straight after the show. We had missed the last bus and train home, so, at great expense, we had to get a taxi home from Leeds to Bilton.

My mother was strict and narrow-minded and did not allow me to go to the weekly 'Bilton hop' but she did allow me to join the youth club at Bar Chapel as she went to the services in the chapel on a Sunday. (Bar Chapel on Skipton Road was named after the nearby Bilton toll bar and not a pub.) So on Friday nights Christine and I went to the youth club run by a lovely chap called Don Johnson and most of the members went across the road afterwards and had a Pepsi in the café. On Saturday evenings some of us went into town to the cinema and the trip used up most of my weekly pocket money of five shillings. The return bus fare was 10d and the cinema ticket was 3s 9d which left me with 5d for the rest of the week. Some of the older youth club members were working so it was not so bad for them, but it was worth it to see Elvis in films such as *Blue Hawaii*.

One Friday night we went on a coach to London so that we could attend the Methodist Association of Youth Clubs annual convention in the Royal Albert Hall. We unsuccessfully tried to sleep overnight on the coach, and eventually Carole climbed onto the luggage rack and slept there. After spending the day in London we all congregated in the Royal Albert Hall. The hall was bursting with young people and our group were in a row quite high up where we could see the tiers lower down. The sound of thousands of young enthusiastic voices all singing together was amazing. It flowed round the tiers of seats like waves and made the hairs on my arms stand on end because it was so awe-inspiring.

Tired after our long day and sleepless night, we went on the coach to Dartford and waited in the church hall to be chosen by local families, like the evacuees had done. A distinguished gentleman chose Christine and I and drove us to his family's lovely bungalow where his wife gave us scallops in shells and a cup of tea. Of course Christine and I had no idea how to eat them, so we sipped our tea each waiting for the other to start. Finally the lady showed us that we scooped them out with a spoon and then we gratefully retired to a lovely bedroom with twin beds where their daughters usually slept. Next morning we set off again armed with delicious sandwiches for our lunch. They were a very hospitable family.

We put on the pantomime *Mother Goose* at Christmas and I was given a leading role, in spite of my protestations. Despite being a fluent reader

I could not read the lines clearly because I would not wear my damned glasses, so I think Don was under the impression that I could not read and I was eventually given the job of prompt.

*

Britain, the United States and Russia had been exploding hydrogen and atomic bombs during the late 1940s and 1950s, and Britain had plans to build twelve atomic power stations. There was growing concern among the general public about a nuclear war and the Campaign for Nuclear Disarmament was formed in 1958. A fifty-mile protest march was organised from London to the Atomic Weapons Research Establishment at Aldermaston, Berkshire. People from all walks of life supported the CND. I well remember the Ban the Bomb marches and the CND symbol.

In 1961 the Soviets and East Germans built a wall around West Berlin to stop the exodus of East Germans to the West. In October 1962 the Soviet Union was discovered to be secretly installing nuclear missiles in Cuba, only ninety miles from the Florida coast. Calculations were that if nuclear weapons were used all human beings in the northern hemisphere could perish. Alarming negotiations by the first telephone hotline between President John F. Kennedy in Washington and the Soviet premier Nikita Khrushchev in Moscow took place. Eventually Khrushchev removed the missiles from Cuba and Kennedy removed the US nuclear missiles which were already in Turkey. The Cuban Missile Crisis of 1962 was the closest we have been to a Third World War.

But in 1963 there was still great fear that Britain would suffer a nuclear attack and the government issued warnings. We were all told that we would receive four minutes' warning of an attack and everyone joked about what they would do in four minutes. RAF Fylingdales in the bleak North York Moors is a radar base built in 1962 as part of the intelligence-sharing arrangements between the USA and the UK and part of the Ballistic Missile Early Warning System (BMEWS) and we would receive our four-minute warning from there.

RAF Fylingdales consisted of three forty-metre-diameter 'golfballs' or radomes similar to RAF Menwith Hill near Harrogate. Appropriately the Fylingdales' motto is '*Vigilamus*', meaning 'We are watching'. When it was built there were protests from communities in Whitby saying that it was a blot on the landscape, but over the years it became a landmark and tourist attraction. Coach trips went to see the site, and postcards were made of the radomes, but there was a blank space on Ordnance Survey maps, as with other sites of military sensitivity, because of security during the Cold War, but the Russians knew all about the sites. After the 1980s and the fall of the Iron Curtain, the Russians released Soviet maps in glorious detail of ninety-two British sites of strategic importance.

When the radomes at Fylingdales were dismantled and replaced by a tetrahedron (pyramid) structure between 1989 and 1992 there was an outcry again from the locals because they did not want to lose the golf balls! RAF Fylingdales still searches for missiles and now has a second objective: space surveillance. The modern facility has a 360-degree range, can see up to 3000 nautical miles, and has been able to track a spanner that an astronaut dropped!

In 1963 Her Majesty's Stationery Office issued a booklet advising householders about what would happen and instructions on how to protect ourselves in a nuclear attack. The advice was to have a fall-out room in a cellar or a cupboard under the stairs and stock it with mattresses, cooking utensils, tinned food, water, torch, radio, clock, books and first aid equipment. Also in the fall-out room we should construct a 'core' thick-walled shelter, and put sandbags on the outside of the fall-out room. The government must have thought we all had huge under-stair cupboards. In case it was necessary to be moved from our shelter we should pack a suitcase with a blanket, change of clothing and some food, and take a coat and gloves. Wardens or the police would tell us when it was safe to go outside and we should wear stout shoes or gumboots. All this seems unbelievable now and these measures would be absolutely hopeless anyway. In 1982 Raymond Briggs published *When the Wind Blows*, an ironic comic-book-style story about an elderly couple's travails during a nuclear explosion. (Raymond Briggs also illustrated the picture book *The Snowman* which is shown on TV each Christmas.)

*

The Cavern Club in Liverpool was inspired by Le Caveau de la Huchette jazz club in Paris. The cellar of a fruit warehouse in Liverpool was used as an air raid shelter in the Second World War and opened in January 1957 as a jazz club and then as a hangout for skiffle groups, as the 2is was. First performing at the Cavern Club, followed by stints in Hamburg, the Beatles were taking the world by storm. John, Paul, George and Ringo released the single 'Love Me Do' in October 1962, then 'Please Please Me', released in January 1963, became their first No. 1 record.

A lot of acts appeared at the Royal Hall in Harrogate and the Beatles performed there in March 1963, but I did not see them. A string of hits followed, written by band members Paul McCartney and John Lennon. Beatlemania had arrived in the UK and then in the USA where it erupted on a tour in 1964. The 'Fab Four', as they were known, even inspired a hairstyle. They wore their hair in the mop-top style which was copied on both sides of the Atlantic. When the Beatles sang at concerts nobody could hear them because the crowd was screaming so much. Over the years their innovative musical style evolved to include a broad variety of pop music. On 8 December 1980 John Lennon was shot and killed outside the Dakota Apartments in New York City by Mark David Chapman, triggering an outpouring of grief. At least three Beatles fans committed suicide in the days after his death. The Beatles were the best-selling band in history and they inspired musicians worldwide.

*

There have been generations of immigrants to Great Britain, from the Romans, Vikings, Irish, Huguenots, Indians, Africans and many others. The British Nationality Act of 1948 gave British citizenship to all people living in Commonwealth countries, and full rights of entry and settlement in Britain. In 1948 the ship *Empire Windrush* brought 492 immigrants to Britain from Jamaica. This began a wave of migration from the Caribbean to the UK for people looking for work and seeking a better life. They were often met with a chilly reception, both from the weather and the British people, and were regularly turned away from accommodation because of the colour of their skin. Many were employed by London Transport and in the nursing profession. We have a friend, Gloria, who came from Barbados in 1955. Britain was short of nurses, and doctors went over to the Caribbean to recruit staff. Gloria was a student nurse and she applied, was chosen, and came over here when she was twenty-one years old to complete her training. She recalls that she stayed in a dormitory at the hospital and the matron came and switched the lights off at 10pm sharp.

I do not remember having any black or Asian children in either my primary or secondary schools. Harrogate being a non-industrial town meant that we did not have many foreign families. The nearby industrial towns of Bradford and Leeds had foreign workers. In Britain we were lucky that there was no conflict regarding segregated education as in the United States, although there has always been racial hostility. The black Americans who had been stationed in Britain during the Second World War were surprised that they could use the same pavements, toilets, pubs and cinemas as white people. The horrors of the death camps in Europe highlighted the insanity of scientific racism, but racism still existed in the USA. Segregation in education was made illegal in the USA by the US Supreme Court in 1954, but little changed. In 1957 nine African-Americans enrolled in the previously all-white Little Rock Central High School in Arkansas. Orval Faubus, the Governor of Arkansas, ordered the National Guard to prevent the black students from entering the school. There was also a hostile white crowd. President Dwight D. Eisenhower intervened and federalised the Arkansas National Guard, then sent in the 101st Airborne Division (without its black soldiers) to protect the black students.

In 1963 Governor George Wallace, flanked by a group of state troopers, blocked two African-Americans from entering the University of Alabama. Again the President of the United States, now John F. Kennedy, federalised the Alabama National Guard and the two students, Vivian Malone and James Hood, were allowed to enter and enrol. We saw and read this in the news, but it seemed so far-removed to me from education in Britain. It was vitally important in the United States.

*

In my final year at Harrogate Grammar School we had rock 'n' roll sessions in Miss Duckworth's prized gym hall on Friday lunchtimes, to which only the fifth forms and above were allowed. The younger pupils climbed on the stone wall outside to watch through the windows, as we had done. For 3d we danced in our gym shoes to music from records on a record player, and practised our jiving. Shirley could throw me over her shoulders and through her legs! I could not do it now. We jived in threes as well, and did the cha-cha-cha.

Although I was listening to pop music a lot, I was revising for my GCEs in 1963 which I sat in June in the main school hall. I achieved good passes in English, Maths, French, Biology and Art. I did not take German and narrowly failed History. Headmaster Ernie Hill pursued high academic excellence and the B-stream students were often written off, especially girls. I did not want to continue in the sixth form but would have liked to go to art school. That was out of the question in my family because I was a girl and did not need further education, so in July I left the grammar school whose former pupils included First World War Victoria Cross holders Donald Simpson Bell and Archie Cecil Thomas White.

Donald Bell had attended St. Peter's Primary School as well as Harrogate Grammar School. After going to Westminster College he became a teacher in Starbeck, then a professional footballer. When war broke out he joined the West Yorkshire Regiment and was promoted to Lance Corporal, then he was commissioned into the Green Howards. For his conspicuous bravery on 5 July 1916 at Horseshoe Trench, Somme he was awarded the Victoria Cross. He was killed in action on 10 July without knowing he had won the nation's highest military honour.

Archie White was a temporary captain in the 6th Battalion, Alexandra, Princess of Wales's Own Yorkshire Regiment, later known as the Green Howards. In France, for several days, he and his troops held a position against heavy fire, then he led a counter-attack which finally cleared the enemy. He eventually achieved the rank of Colonel and died in May 1971. 'To have two school friends both awarded the V.C. on the same battlefield is probably unique in British military history,' said Richard Leake who wrote a book, *A Breed Apart*, about the two brave men.

For my achievement in the GCEs Mum and Dad bought me a pale blue Bush transistor radio, a 'tranny'. They were sold in pale blue or cream. I now have a cream digital radio which is a copy of the old Bush radio.

A Civil Servant

On 19 August 1963 I ceased being a schoolgirl and became a member of the British working class: a civil servant. By now I had learnt that a civil servant was not a domestic servant as I had thought when Granny Hodgson had suggested several years ago that I should be a civil servant when I grew up. I was horrified at the time as I did not want a lowly job as a servant working all hours helping to look after a house and family.

So after finishing school near the end of July I left my school friends and did not see most of them again, only a few who became civil servants like me. After a week's family holiday in Blackpool I caught the special bus from Bilton to St. George's Road to start work at 8.30am. The regular bus only went into Harrogate town centre but St. George's Road was about a mile or two further on so we had a special bus, as I had when I went to grammar school. Along the route our red single-decker bus trundled up Bilton Lane, along King Edward's Drive and Skipton Road, down steep King's Road, across the junction at the foot of Parliament Street near the Royal Baths and the Royal Hall. It then climbed up Cold Bath Road, along Arthur's Avenue and past my old grammar school to the junction of 'the huts' and Harrogate cricket ground. Here the bus disgorged its motley crowd into the biting wind. Harrogate is a windy place and the site at St. George's Road was elevated and exposed. There were five blocks in the complex. The bus stopped at the entrance to the site near block 1. I worked in block 5 so still had about a five- or ten-minute walk until I reached the relative warmth of the concrete corridor.

Most people viewed the Civil Service as being a cushy job which involved a lot of tea drinking and being employed from 9am to 5pm Monday to Friday.

Actually one of the reasons I wanted to be a civil servant was because we had Saturdays off like school. But the hours were 8.30am until 5.30pm with an hour for lunch. They were set times which everybody worked. We signed in the clocking-on book when we arrived and all signed out at the end of the day. There were no flexible working hours in those days. People worked set hours with or without overtime. Shops had a half-day closing, and in Harrogate the shops closed on a Wednesday afternoon and did not open on Sundays.

*

So at work I stopped being 'Christine' or 'Christine Wardman' and was now 'Miss Wardman' which sounded very formal and grown up. I was sixteen years old, two months short of my seventeenth birthday. We had several forms to complete including the Official Secrets Act and, if my memory serves me correctly, a form to state that I would not flick elastic bands around the office!

I was assigned to Scottish Ledgers in the Post Office Savings Bank at 'the huts' which were temporary terrapin buildings erected during the Second World War to be used as hospitals if necessary. There was a central corridor with long rooms going off each side at intervals for wards. Some windows still had blackout blinds. There were two sections or offices in each room.

The ledger cards were a copy of the person's bank book with corresponding entries of deposits and withdrawals which were made at post offices around the country. Forces Savings were in other offices. Forces personnel saved some of their salary in post office accounts. I was told that, during the Second World War when ships went down, the Post Office Savings Bank books went down with their owners and sometimes the relatives did not know about the accounts so the money was still there.

Actually, to start with, work was not unlike school. There were six new entrants at Clerical Officer level in Scottish Ledgers. We had passed at least five General Certificate of Education (GCE) 'O' Levels which meant we could enter the Civil Service at Clerical Officer grade, above Clerical Assistants and Machinists. Sylvia Watson taught us how to examine bank books and check the entries against the ledger cards. We calculated interest by how many whole pounds were in each account each month of the year. All this was manual of course, long before computers were used extensively.

In the UK early computers were developed from technological advances during the Second World War at centres such as Bletchley Park. English Electric Ltd. was one of the early British computer manufacturers. Probably the first digital computer to undertake business data processing was LEO (Lyons Electronic Office) in 1951 installed by Joseph Lyons and Co. to handle the company's accounts and logistics. Lyons was best known for their chain of tea shops and Lyons Corner Houses in the West End of London. LEO was programmed to factor in the weather forecast to determine the fresh produce carried by Lyons delivery vans. Oxford graduate Margaret Thatcher (née Roberts) worked as a research chemist for J. Lyons and Co. in Hammersmith food laboratory as part of a team developing emulsifiers for ice cream. She worked there to support herself before becoming a Member of Parliament and eventually Britain's first woman Prime Minister.

The first computers were room-sized and often became overheated. They used vacuum tubes, then transistors, followed by the transistor chip. So before we had computers in the Civil Service we used pens, pencils and pieces of paper to write the figures down, add up the column and calculate the interest. The annual interest rate never varied for years. It was 2.5% or 6d in the pound, that is six old pence or two and a half new pence now. At the Yorkshire Penny Bank, later the Yorkshire Bank, the interest was 1.75%. That's where I had my small savings account from school.

We learnt in a relaxed atmosphere in a side room with Sylvia as our teacher and we were not very serious so there was a lot of laughing while learning. We had a pep talk by a Higher Executive Officer and I asked him why, as youngsters, our pay was so low. His answer was, 'We want to attract the right calibre of staff.' One perk was that civil servants retired at sixty years of age and not at sixty-five as some occupations. That was a long way off for me though.

It seemed a pity when we finished our initial three-week training course and went to work in the main office. Even that was not so bad because the machinists walked around the office and there was a lot of clacking from the machines so it wasn't all quiet and serious. We were a mixed bunch: some younger, a few married women and several boring old farts, men of course. Not everyone was stuffy and formal, with a few characters when I got to know them.

Laura worked in our office for a while as a Clerical Officer. She was very intelligent but was actually one of those people who may be academically clever but without any common sense; that's when I realised that the two don't necessarily go together. She lolloped into the office with her head wobbling from side to side like the toy nodding dogs in the backs of cars. Her head seemed always in the clouds and she was in a world of her own, sitting on a desk swinging her legs and singing softly to herself.

After learning the basics of examining books and calculating interest I moved on to tray duty, allocating work to the machinists and correcting mistakes. The amounts of money on deposit slips and withdrawal slips, which arrived daily from post offices in bundles, were keyed onto adding machines on the corresponding ledger cards. Then the slips were totalled up by another machinist and the two figures should match. If not we had to go through the batch to see where the discrepancy or discrepancies were. Sometimes ledger cards were misfiled and I enjoyed doing a bit of detective work discovering where they had been filed. Our office had Scottish Ledgers H to K which meant streets or towns beginning with that letter. For instance, we had Kelso, Kelty, Kilbirnie, Kincardine, Kirkcudbright (pronounced Kirkoobrie). We also had a large section devoted to Hope Street, Edinburgh and Hope Street, Glasgow. So if we could not find a card which should have been in Hope Street, Edinburgh we obviously looked in the corresponding address in Hope Street, Glasgow. This was not the case if Laura had been anywhere near the ledger cards. Oh no. A card could be anywhere, absolutely anywhere at all. We spent ages searching for lost cards in these instances but usually had to give up and hoped they would turn up at some time. We even wondered if she wandered off and put them in the trays in another office. Eventually Laura drifted off as she had drifted in. I don't know where she came from or where she went but the office was more orderly after her departure.

Roger Johnson was a few years older than me. He was quite irreverent to the older COs in the office, calling them by their first names. Everyone tolerated Roger. When I started work the Profumo scandal had been simmering and was being reported in all its various revelations. John Profumo was the Secretary of State for War in Harold Macmillan's Conservative government. At a party in July 1961 at Cliveden, which was the country estate of Lord Astor, John Profumo was introduced to nineteen-year-old would-be model Christine Keeler by Stephen Ward. Stephen Ward was an osteopath and artist with connections to aristocracy and the underworld. Keeler was swimming naked and was introduced to Profumo. Over the weekend there was lots of frolicking around the pool. Also at this weekend party was a Russian military attaché, Captain Yevgeny Ivanov, who was in a relationship with Christine Keeler. Ivanov was known by MI5 to be a Russian intelligence officer. With Stephen Ward's encouragement John Profumo began an affair with Christine Keeler.

Keeler and her friend Mandy Rice-Davies became indiscreet as their private lives unravelled and the media became involved.

When the Profumo-Keeler-Ivanov affair was first revealed there was much public interest and suspicion that there could have been a national security risk. In March 1963 Profumo made a personal statement to the House of Commons denying any impropriety. He lied and was forced to admit the truth a few weeks later. He resigned in disgrace from the government and from Parliament.

In June 1963 Stephen Ward was charged with immorality offences. He was abandoned by his erstwhile society friends and exposed to the contempt and hostility of prosecuting counsel and judge. He was convicted on two counts of living off immoral earnings. However, before the verdict was announced, Ward took an overdose of sleeping pills and died three days later on 3 August 1963. At the time his death was accepted as suicide. Later theories suggested that he could have been killed on orders of MI5.

In October 1963 Harold Macmillan resigned as Prime Minister. The scandal contributed to the defeat of the Conservative government by Labour in the 1964 general election.

Years later I did a tour of Cliveden and saw the notorious swimming pool, and the guide recounted the sordid events of the 1960s. It was an ignominious episode which still lives on in the memories of our generation. There have been TV programmes, films and plays about the scandal and the people involved.

So, on the strength of this scandal and publicity, and as my first name was Christine, I became Christine Keeler for a while to Roger Johnson.

*

A smart and dapper Clerical Officer, Dick Musgrove, was a stickler for detail and correctness. His usual phrase was 'a place for everything and everything in its place' which is not a bad mantra. Dick was disappointed as he was still a Clerical Officer after working all his life and was near retirement. Previously he had refused to move to a government department in Chesterfield. You had to move to get on in the Civil Service. In Harrogate the only way to get promoted was 'dead men's shoes'. Dick and I did the *Daily Telegraph* crossword together at lunchtimes.

Harry Watson was another character. With grizzled grey hair, weather-beaten countenance and absent-minded air he looked about seventy years old but of course wouldn't be more than sixty. One day he had examined a pile of bank books and one was missing. We each signed for a batch of bank books and the number had to be checked before they were posted out. This was in case of fraud. If you had someone's bank book you could go to a post office and withdraw the money. We all looked high and low for this bank book, under tables, in cupboards, re-counted bundles, everywhere. Eventually Harry remembered: he had put it under the cushion on his chair to flatten out the envelope. Panic over.

We had a tea break morning and afternoon. That is not strictly true. The machinists were allowed a ten-minute tea break so they could sit down as they were on their feet most of the day. Clerical Officers drank their tea or coffee at their desks while working. A canteen worker came in to each office and shouted, 'Tea's up!' as she brought in a large urn of boiling water. Our cups were lined up ready on a Formica-topped table in preparation.

As Clerical Officers we received our pay at the end of each calendar month, twelve payments per year. Machinists received their pay weekly. There were no cheques or credit cards then. Our pay was handed to us in cash in a brown paper envelope. At the end of the month a call went up in the office, 'Pay's here', and we trouped into the corridor and stood in line to collect our pay from two members of Pay Section who had the money in a satchel. As with everything else we signed our name in a big ledger. The names were in alphabetical order. As my surname was Wardman it was just above Watson on the list. I could see that I received about £24 per month, half of Harry Watson's £48. My first full month's pay for September 1963 was £26 5s 0d gross. This was before decimalisation which took place on 15 February 1971 when our currency changed, the pound being retained but divided into one hundred new pence. In 1963 our currency was still pounds, shillings and pence. So in 1963 my annual salary was £315 gross. My pay wasn't great but I hoped I would get a good Civil Service pension when I retired. It was a non-contributory pension scheme which meant that was taken into consideration when the pay scales were calculated. I never received a Civil Service pension, though, as I left to start my family after eight and a half years' service and if you left before ten years' service and you were less than fifty years of age you received nothing.

Pay scales were very long back then; you reached your 'max' when you were thirty-two years old. Starting pay was at the level for your age unless you came in over age twenty-five when you started at that level. So in September 1963 I entered the pay scale at age sixteen. I did not pay income tax as I was under eighteen, but my National Insurance contribution was £1 11s 8d, so my take home pay was £24 13s 4d for the month. After marriage, when I actually left the Civil Service to have a baby when I was almost twenty-five years old, I had learned all the Clerical Officer jobs available including teaching new staff and also balancing the figures for the total year for our whole section. After eight and a half years I still did not receive the pay an untrained officer received as their starting pay if they were over twenty-five.

Several years after beginning work, as technology moved forward, we were offered a cash incentive to have our salary paid directly into a bank account. This removed the security risk of large amounts of cash being transported around by pay office staff on pay days.

Until we were eighteen years old we had one day a week at a 'day release' college in Harrogate for further education, the old Harrogate Technical College on Haywra Crescent where Geoffrey had attended from the age of thirteen. It was now the Harrogate Institute of Further Education and I went each week on Fridays. Lessons were totally different from school, and we were treated as students rather than school children. Mr Grundy, a kindly, diminutive chap with thick white hair taught us English and often quoted begged questions. I recall his phrase, 'Have you stopped beating your wife yet?' as an example of a begged question. We had tutors for Maths, Geography and Current Affairs. I was shocked when we did examples of mortgage repayments and realised that the amount repaid was three times more than the original loan at the end of the usual twenty-five-year term. But we all aspired to owning our own homes and that meant taking out a mortgage.

At lunchtime we were let loose into the shops and restaurants in town. Susan Armstrong, Diane Hardy, Christine Ball and I went to the Blue Sky Chinese restaurant to use our lunch vouchers, hoping we wouldn't be eating cats, as was rumoured, in these new restaurants. Then we went to the old market hall to listen to records at Robell's Music Box. We crushed into booths to hear the 'B' side of singles to see if they were worth buying, but often it was just to listen to the Beatles' latest record, or Elvis, or Helen Shapiro.

I went to the Friday classes for a year, until I was eighteen and, surprisingly, won the annual prize for the student who had gained most benefit from the classes. My prize was a book, and I chose a cookery book, hoping I would learn to be a better cook than my mum.

One Friday an event happened which stunned the world. It was one of those I-remember-where-I-was moments. About 12.30pm on 22 November 1963, the 35th President of the United States, John Fitzgerald Kennedy, was assassinated as he rode next to his wife Jacqueline in a motorcade in Dallas, Texas. The time was around 6.30pm in the UK on a day when I had been to my day release class, and the news of the shooting soon spread around the globe. A description of the suspect was radioed to police officers, one of whom was J. D. Tippit who saw someone who fitted the description and called him over to his patrol car. The suspect was Lee Harvey Oswald who shot the police officer four times and killed him. Soon afterwards Oswald was arrested in a theatre and charged with the murders of President Kennedy and Officer Tippit, but he was never brought to trial because Oswald himself was shot and killed by nightclub owner Jack Ruby while being transferred to Dallas County Jail. This was filmed live on American television. President Kennedy's body was flown back to Washington DC and his state funeral took place on Monday 25 November after which he was laid to rest in Arlington National Cemetery in Virginia. After a ten-month investigation by the Warren Commission it was concluded that Lee Harvey Oswald acted alone in shooting the President, and that Jack Ruby also acted alone when he killed Oswald. Controversy and conspiracy theories still surround the assassination and in 1992 there was a film called *JFK* which renewed public interest in it.

Racial discrimination was one of the most pressing domestic issues in the USA in the 1960s. President Kennedy had verbally supported racial integration and civil rights and appointed many black people to office during his presidency. He intervened when the Alabama Governor George

Wallace stopped the two African-American students from attending the University of Alabama. That evening Kennedy had given his famous Civil Rights Address on national television and radio, to provide equal access to public schools and other facilities, and greater protection of voting rights.

On 28 August 1963 Martin Luther King made his 'I have a dream' speech to a crowd of over 100,000 mostly African-Americans gathered for the 'March on Washington for Jobs and Freedom'. Although thousands of troops were placed on standby, it was a peaceful demonstration and there were no arrests. Kennedy had watched King's speech on TV and was very impressed and invited the march leaders to the White House. The Civil Rights Act of 1964 included Kennedy's proposals. On 4 April 1968 Martin Luther King himself was shot and killed, while standing on the balcony of the Lorraine Motel in Memphis, by James Earl Ray. I visited the spot on a trip to Memphis in 2015.

*

Mrs Sterling, a married lady in our office, was a pleasure to work alongside, as was Miss Fox who was a very accurate worker. I thought that if I had a business there were certain members of staff I would like to employ. These ladies were two of them.

Our supervisor was a Higher Clerical Officer who sat in his chair and surveyed all before him. Actually everyone knew their own jobs and the office seemed to run itself. There were no meetings, as companies do nowadays. Manuals detailed our jobs and procedures, and experienced staff were there if we encountered unusual problems. The HCO signed our few handwritten letters which were then sent off to a typing pool. Most instances were covered by standard letters which were kept in wooden pigeonholes on our desks. When the HCO was bored he used to amble out of the office and go and talk to another HCO in another office.

George Sheffield was my first HCO, followed by George Westwood, who was my HCO when I won the prize for my further education studies. A young man in my office was awarded the prize for the best Wednesday student of the year and George Westwood was very pleased that he had two prize-winners in his office. He was a good boss if you worked well, and I did, so I liked him.

Then came Miss Perry, a chinless wonder with her grey hair in a 1950s roll at the back of her head tied with a fine hair net. She had relocated from London and kept her London working hours of one hour less per day, given to Londoners as it was deemed they had longer distances to travel to work than the rest of the country. She also retained her 'London weighting' which was an extra allowance on top of salary designed to help workers with the higher cost of living in the capital. These amounted to more than my salary. Rumour had it that Miss Perry bought her clothes from jumble sales and it was not surprising by the looks of her.

Iris Tyson was a Clerical Officer who bustled about and looked very efficient. She rushed her 'advanced interest' calculations which we did in batches on ledger cards during quieter periods. We part-calculated the annual interest so that there was not so much work to do at the end of the year. When the bank books came in for examination the interest was calculated again and checked against the ledger card. If there was a large discrepancy it was rechecked by Central Duty, an experienced officer. A lot of discrepancies were in Iris Tyson's handwriting. George Sheffield thought Iris was a great worker. He was not aware that most of her calculations were wrong.

Elsie Smith was a machinist in our section. She was called Mrs Cheese and Onion because of the body odour she left behind as she wafted around the office. And, as she leaned over the trays, her ample thighs and the tops of her stockings were a sight to behold. It was enough to put us off our tea break. Friday was her usual day off sick when she went into town shopping. George Sheffield sympathised with her illnesses. He was not a very good judge.

Lionel, known as Li Li, worked in a different office. One hot, sultry and sunny afternoon (yes, it can get hot in Yorkshire) he drifted into our section. All was quiet as the machinists had finished their listings, and Li Li flamboyantly waved his long-nailed hands in the air and exclaimed, 'Oh, it's so hot. I wish I had worn my grass skirt today,' and drifted out again followed by amused and surprised stares. He frequented the Gardeners Arms pub in Bilton in the evenings and was usually in the company of females who shared his interests of clothes, make-up and jewellery. After sipping copious amounts of ale he wandered home through the fields, collecting hedgehogs as he went to place in his garden.

*

In December 1963 Dad joined the third of households in Britain when he bought a car, an Austin A40 with a silver-grey body and black roof, registration 11LNN.

By 1955 about two thirds of Europe's oil passed through the Suez Canal in Egypt. Supplies of fuel from the Middle East were blocked when Egyptian President Garnal Abdel Nasser took over the running of the Suez Canal. The Suez Crisis of 1956 was the invasion of Egypt by Israel, followed by Britain and France to regain Western control of the canal after its nationalisation. The invasion was very successful from a military point of view, but was a disaster politically, drawing international criticism, diplomatic and financial pressure, especially from the United States. The invading troops withdrew and Britain and France were humiliated. Petrol was rationed in Britain which led to panic buying. The motor car industry was hit with a reduction in the number of passenger cars being built.

Because of the rise in the standard of living and the reduction in car prices by improved mass manufacture, there was a boom in car ownership during the 1950s and 1960s. People were lured by the 'freedom of the open road', and petrol was available again. The south-north motorway, the M1, was being built connecting London to Leeds. So, from December 1963, our little family did not have to rely on Uncle Tom for our weekend trips around Yorkshire and for our holidays.

*

The day before the Christmas holiday we were allowed a long lunch break and a lot of people went into town to the pubs. The Alexander was popular. Then a lot of inebriated people straggled back to work in the afternoon. I remember one year in particular. Football pool syndicates were popular and just before Christmas one group on the site had a very big win on Littlewoods Pools. One young lad in the group was just twenty-one years old and with his winnings he bought his girlfriend an engagement ring and put a deposit down on a house. That Christmas he celebrated and got so drunk he was taken to hospital and had to have his stomach pumped to rid him of the poison alcohol.

One HCO in the next office tried to stop us going out for our Christmas lunchtime one year. He was a member of the religious group the Plymouth Brethren who did not celebrate Christmas and he started preaching to us telling us what sinners we were to celebrate Christmas. He did not succeed.

Another colleague, big, affable Joe Welsh, was a member of the Magic Circle and did tricks in the office at Christmas when we were back from the pubs. He stood on a chair and held a milk bottle full of water upside down. Magically it did not spill out. He made a great ceremony for me to do it next and of course the water spilled out all over the floor as he had slipped the transparent stopper off the bottle. After a few drinks we all thought this was hilarious.

These antics were not in keeping with the staid Civil Service, so eventually we were all given the afternoon off before Christmas to avoid any unseemly behaviour on Crown property.

*

In January we signed for our annual leave. We had two weeks' paid leave each year, one summer week and either one winter week or five days taken as days off or half-days. We each filed in seniority in to the Higher Clerical Officer's room to sign for our summer week. Only one person was allowed leave each week, so if someone senior had signed for that week that was it, you could not have the same week.

Overtime was available at the beginning of the year when we did the 'completion ints'. This is when we usually found Laura's misfiled ledger cards! Monday to Friday we could work from 5.30pm to 9.30pm at time-and-a-half. If you did this all week then you qualified for double time on Saturday mornings from 8.30am to 12.30pm, otherwise that was time-and-a-half too. I worked Monday to Friday evenings for about eight weeks during January and February until all the calculations had been completed. They were long days in the middle of winter with no special bus to take us home after overtime, so I walked across West Park Stray to the bus station in town to get a bus home to Bilton.

One day it snowed heavily during the day. When I had set off for work in my pencil-slim skirt and high heels it had been a clear morning. By the end of overtime there was too much snow for me to walk into town. Reggie West offered me a lift on his 125cc motorbike which I accepted. I put on my coat and hitched up my skirt. Reggie was ready and I thought I had better not keep him waiting by rummaging through my bag for my gloves, so I swung my leg over the motorbike and grabbed him round the waist. The black sky was above us and the white snow-covered road sped by underneath us. As the freezing wind whistled past us my hands became colder and colder. I did not realise how cold it would be. When I arrived home my hands were numb. I don't know how I managed to negotiate the door with freezing hands. They painfully thawed out until the circulation returned.

The Mid-1960s

By now I was going out with Charles (Chas) who played cricket at Bilton Cricket Club. You could say that I scored in more ways than one at BCC. We both worked at 'the huts', but not in the same block: I worked in Scottish Ledgers in Block 5, and Chas worked in Forces Savings in Block 3.

Friday evenings in winter were when we played badminton at Rossett Sports Centre where the Civil Service hired courts. There were quite a few good badminton players (but not me) and Anne and Bill Behagg were two of them. Their son John had been in the same class as me at St. Peter's Primary School. Badminton evenings were similar to working overtime, in that Chas and I had to walk across the Stray to the bus station to catch the bus home to Bilton on cold dark winter nights. It was either that, or wait ages in the cold for the bus from Leeds to Harrogate bus station, and then the bus home.

On Saturdays in winter Chas played football for the Post Office Savings team; the penalty at the end was the unhygienic communal bath. Then in the evenings we usually went to the cinema so that he could rest his battered and bruised legs from kicks he had received in the afternoon. We caught the bus into town and I clip-clopped in my high heels, often stopping abruptly when I caught my stiletto in a gap in the pavement, and we joined other couples to view the latest films. The Gaumont and the St. James cinemas, prime sites both on Cambridge Street in the centre of Harrogate, had closed down by 1960 to make way for the new Littlewoods store. The out-of-town Ritz closed as a cinema in October 1962 and reopened as a bingo hall. So, from the cinema hey-day, there were only two cinemas now to choose from: the ABC Regal and the Odeon.

In the cinema the atmosphere was filled with smoke and Old Spice aftershave. We saw James Bond films, and 'kitchen sink' dramas such as *Saturday Night and Sunday Morning* and *This Sporting Life*. Despite it being a box office success in 1963, with number 1 hit records from the film, we walked out of *Summer Holiday* starring Cliff Richard as we both thought it was rubbish. Sorry, Cliff, you can't win 'em all. After the cinema we had fish and chips from Tower Street fish shop and walked home eating them out of newspaper, the best way, or ate them at the bus shelter near the library gardens while waiting for the bus. Then we realised we could eat at the fish restaurant and starting having our regular order of 'one of each, tea, bread and butter twice'. In those days there was not a choice of chicken or sausage or even haddock. It was just cod and chips, so in Yorkshire the order was 'one of each'. We did not even get Yorkshire caviar (mushy peas, ha, ha!) or curry sauce which we would have now. But we enjoyed our meal which I could not eat at 10.30pm now as it is too late. In those days our staple diet seemed to be something and chips.

*

In the news on 8 August 1963 we had learned of an audacious and sensational £2.6 million robbery in Buckinghamshire from a Royal Mail night train travelling from Glasgow to London. This amount would be equivalent to about £49 million today and the robbery became known as the Great Train Robbery. The gang of sixteen robbers stopped the train, coshed the driver, and stole 120 mailbags of High Value Packages (HVPs), then hid out at Leatherslade Farm which they had bought two months earlier. There they counted out the proceeds, mostly £1 and £5 notes, and divided it into seventeen shares, with smaller sums of money for associates. The full shares were about £150,000 each (about £2.65 million today). From listening to their radio, tuned in to the police, the gang realised that the police would probably discover the farm much sooner than they had anticipated, so they left earlier than they had intended. They arranged for someone to carry out a thorough clean-up of the farm and then set fire to it. That did not happen and the police found the hideout along with incriminating evidence. Fingerprints were found on a Monopoly set which the robbers had used for a game, but with real money! Most of the gang members were caught soon after and brought to trial in January 1964. Seven of the ringleaders were sentenced in April to thirty years' imprisonment, which was longer than many sentences given to murderers. Subsequently some of the prisoners escaped but had to use much of their ill-gotten gains to evade capture. Some gang members fled abroad and had plastic surgery and squandered their money. Most were caught but the bulk of the stolen money was never recovered.

Although the Great Train Robbers seriously injured the train driver during the robbery, they were often romanticised and regarded as folk heroes, with many books, films and TV programmes written about them. There was a certain amount of sympathy within the British public because of the long sentences they received.

Government figures showed that the average weekly wage in the UK was £16 in 1964, so the train robbery netted an unbelievable amount of money to most people. My net weekly pay as a Clerical Officer was about £6.

At lunchtime in the canteen I enjoyed corned beef and chips sometimes, but in 1964 there was a typhoid outbreak in Aberdeen which was traced to contaminated tinned corned beef made by Fray Bentos, which had been imported from Argentina to a branch of the Scottish grocery chain William Low. The infected meat then contaminated a meatslicing machine in the William Low shop, leading to the spread of the disease. More than 400 people in Aberdeen were diagnosed with typhoid, and although there were no fatalities, most people in the UK stopped eating corned beef, including me. One of the changes made following the outbreak was the elimination of roller towels in public toilets to prevent the spread of bacteria. This probably led to the use of disposable paper hand towels.

*

In sport in 1964 Cassius Clay (later Muhammad Ali) beat Sonny Liston to win the WBA and WBC heavyweight titles. For a heavyweight boxer he was surprisingly light on his feet and he craved the spotlight, often making up derogatory poetry to taunt his opponents. He is regarded as one of the leading heavyweight boxers of the twentieth century, and one of the most significant and celebrated sports figures. He was also a political activist and refused to be drafted into the US military, citing his religious beliefs and opposition to American involvement in the Vietnam War.

Also in sport, the British team had success at the Summer Olympic Games in Tokyo in 1964 with four gold medals, seven silver medals and one bronze medal in athletics. There were five silver medals in other events making eighteen medals in all and the British news was full of these sports personalities. Welsh Lynn Davies won a gold medal in the men's long jump. Ann Packer won a gold in the women's 800 metres and a silver in the 400 metres. She was engaged to Robbie Brightwell who won a silver medal in the men's 4 x 400 relay, and they got married in December that year. Golden Girl blonde Mary Rand won a gold in the women's long jump, breaking the world record, a silver in the women's pentathlon and a bronze in the women's 4 x 100 relay. She remains the only Great Britain female athlete to win three medals in a single Olympic Games. She was succeeded as Golden Girl of British athletics by her friend and London Olympiades club-mate Lillian Board who was another attractive blonde, a lovely girl who the British people took to their hearts. She was a promising middle-distance runner and achieved a silver medal in the 1968 Summer Olympics in Mexico City, setting a new UK record and missing out on gold by less than a second. This was her first Olympic Games at nineteen years of age. Success came in the 1969 European Championships in Athens when she won two gold medals and was named 'Best Woman Athlete in the Games'. In June 1970 she was still winning races but had stomach pains and was diagnosed with terminal bowel cancer in September. Watching the news on TV we were dismayed as she was flown to West Germany for controversial treatment, but to no avail. The BBC interrupted the evening programme of festivities on Boxing Day with a sombre newsflash announcing her death. She had lost her fight for life at the age of just twenty-two. It was a tragedy for a beautiful and fit young woman who had not reached her potential, but was one of the greatest female athletes of her generation.

Charismatic Donald Campbell broke both the world land and water speed records in 1964 and remains the only person to do so in the same year. At another attempt at a water speed record in January 1967 on Lake Coniston in the Lake District, his rocket-powered *Bluebird* flipped up out of the water in an almost complete somersault, cartwheeled and broke up, killing him instantly. The boat was located on the lake bed the next day but Campbell's body was not found, although his mascot teddy bear Mr Whoppit was recovered among the floating debris. In 2001 the *Bluebird* was raised from the lake bed and Campbell's body was recovered, still wearing the blue nylon overalls. He was buried in Coniston Cemetery on 12 September 2001 but the media coverage of the funeral was overshadowed by the unforgettable 9/11 terror attacks in New York.

*

Teenagers in the UK began listening to 'pirate' radio stations broadcasting from offshore ships or disused forts in international waters. The BBC was regarded as 'frumpy' and wasn't playing pop or rock music. Radio Luxemburg only played records by artists signed to the major record labels such as Decca, Capitol, Parlophone, EMI and Philips, so Irish entrepreneur Ronan O'Rahilly decided to do something about it. He bought a ship and converted it to make broadcasts from studios built behind the ship's bridge. His Radio Caroline started broadcasts to meet the growing demand, with disc jockeys including Simon Dee, Johnnie Walker and Tony Blackburn. Entrepreneurs set up other pirate radio stations and by 1965 had an audience of ten to fifteen million, including me and my friends, although I still listened to *The Top Twenty* on BBC Radio 1 on Sunday lunchtimes and taped some of the tunes on my tape recorder.

The Labour government, under Prime Minister Harold Wilson, brought in the Marine Broadcasting Offences Act of 1967 which effectively closed down most of the offshore radio stations, except Caroline which was forced to close in 1968. Ronan O'Rahilly started a campaign and recruited supporters against the Labour Party and Harold Wilson who was seeking re-election in 1970. This was the first election in which eighteen- to twenty-one-year-olds could vote, and maybe this was overlooked by the government. The youngsters were motivated to strike back at the politicians who had so arrogantly ruined their enjoyment. In any case, Labour had a surprising loss to the Conservatives.

Tony Blackburn has come full circle as he now presents *Sounds of the Sixties* on BBC Radio 2, taking over from veteran DJ Brian Matthew who was summarily retired in February 2017 by new Head of Radio 2, Lewis Carnie. This possibly accelerated Brian Matthew's death on 8 April 2017.

*

We laughed at the bawdy humour in the *Carry On* comedy films starring a host of well-known British actors including Hattie Jacques, Joan Sims, Barbara Windsor, Sid James, Kenneth Williams, Charles Hawtrey, Kenneth Connor, Terry Scott, Bernard Bresslaw, Peter Butterworth and Jim Dale, who usually played the hapless romantic lead. Whatever happened to Jim Dale? Well, let me see. He trained as a dancer and his career includes being a singer, comedy actor, Shakespearean actor, and lyricist for the hit song 'Georgy Girl'; he moved to New York and played 'Barnum' on Broadway; he has recorded all seven Harry Potter audiobooks, creating a staggering 147 different voices for one book; is renowned for performing his own on-screen stunts; has won many awards, and recently performed several one-man shows – *Just Jim Dale*. Gosh!

We also loved watching comedy duo Eric Morecambe and Ernie Wise in *Two of a Kind* on television, followed by *The Morecambe and Wise Show* in 1968. Their Christmas shows were essential viewing, with prime-time viewing figures of more than 20 million, some of the largest in British television history.

*

The final section of Britain's first long-distance footpath, the Pennine Way, was opened in 1965. The path runs from Edale in the Derbyshire Peak District, through the Yorkshire Dales, moors and the backbone of England (the Pennines) to Kirk Yetholm, just inside the Scottish border. It is a tough 267-mile long-distance walk. We have done some of it, but really enjoyed our Dales Way walk along the beautiful River Wharfe in God's Own County in 2013. It was exhilarating and we were grateful for not being attacked by cows, bulls, sheep, or irate farmers, or being cremated by an electric fence.

Another moor became famous in 1965 when Ian Brady and Myra Hindley carried out 'The Moors Murders'. Five children had gone missing, and two of their bodies were discovered on Saddleworth Moor in Lancashire soon after, with a third body discovered more than twenty years later. The murders were reported all over the world and we were all horrified to learn that 'the two sadistic killers of the utmost depravity', as the trial judge called them, had tortured the children and recorded their screams. Because the death penalty had been abolished recently, Brady and Hindley were sentenced to mandatory life imprisonment. Myra Hindley died in 2002, and, after being incarcerated for more than half a century, Ian Brady died in May 2017. The cost to the taxpayer on the detection, trial and imprisonment of these vile individuals has been millions of pounds.

*

On a much brighter note, fashion was in the news and I was wearing the mini-skirt, attributed to Mary Quant. In winter girls were getting chapped knees from the cold, but it was all endured and necessary because of fashion. Yves Saint Laurent brought out the iconic shift dress with graphic lines, white spaces and primary colours. Carnaby Street in London was the centre of independent fashion boutiques and was buzzing and vibrant. Vidal Sassoon created his short, geometric hairstyles, and model Twiggy became an international supermodel and 'The Face of 1966'. Her photo, with big eyes, long eyelashes and short hair, adorned the covers of *Vogue* and *The Tatler*. London was swinging and it seemed that it was all happening there, but fashion and style in Yorkshire was a pale copy.

In 1966 40% of the UK population were under twenty-five; the average weekly wage for women was £12 and for men it was £23; and 96% of people getting married had not lived together. Abortion was illegal, as was male homosexuality (lesbian acts had never been illegal) and being arrested for 'gross indecency' could lead to prison sentences and reputations lost. The brilliant Irish playwright, novelist and poet Oscar Wilde had been imprisoned for two years' hard labour in 1895 for gross indecency with men, and died, broken and impoverished in France in 1900, soon after writing the tragically haunting *The Ballad of Reading Gaol*. Even Alan Turing, the great mathematician, computer genius and Enigma codebreaker had been convicted of gross indecency in 1952, forced to undergo hormone therapy and lost his security clearance. He later apparently committed suicide by eating an apple laced with cyanide, reputedly leading to the inspiration by the Apple technology company of their apple logo showing the bite taken out.

*

Chas and I continued working overtime in winter because by now we were saving to get married. On Sundays I still had roast dinner at home and Dad and I drank our shandy. My mum wasn't very well and was losing her balance and kept dropping things because she couldn't grasp them very well. One lunch break from work when she was walking unsteadily in Woolworths, she overheard a woman say to her friend, 'Look at her. Fancy being drunk already at this time of day.' Understandably this upset my mother greatly, especially as she did not drink anyway. She did not understand why her balance was being affected.

After several tests, including a lumbar puncture, Mum was diagnosed with multiple sclerosis. The doctor said it could have been caused by the shock of Geoffrey's death. She had to leave work at Bettys Café where she was at that time, serving bread and cakes and lifting heavy trays. She did not receive any disability allowance because, like lots of married women, she had been advised to pay the 'small stamp', the reduced National Insurance contributions, which married women could do. The reduced rate meant there are no rights to a pension and no sickness benefit. Most married women were encouraged, or told, to pay the reduced rate, but most were not told of these disadvantages, and my mum was one of them. It was not until near retirement that most of these women learnt that they would get no retirement pension in their own right, even though they had been working for most of their married lives. It was acknowledged that the system was unfair when the reduced rate was stopped for women married on or after 6 April 1977, but the ones already on the reduced rate were not advised, and therefore carried on as before. The loss of pension rights far outweighed any gains they made by paying the small stamp, with no right to buy back lost years. These losses ran into thousands of pounds and were regarded as a scandal when women realised they had not been fully informed.

*

Not only did I watch England win the FIFA World Cup live on TV from Wembley with Chas on Saturday 30 July 1966, we saw it at the cinema too, but I drew the line when it rolled on a second time. So the names of the England team that day should be burned in my memory, and most of them are: Bobby Moore, captain; Gordon Banks, goalie; Jack Charlton, Bobby

Charlton, Nobby Stiles, Alan Ball, Martin Peters and Geoff Hurst. I had forgotten George Cohen, Roger Hunt and Ray Wilson. England won 4-2 in extra time, and the match is remembered for England's only World Cup win, Geoff Hurst's hat-trick (the first one in a World Cup Final), and England's controversial third goal. The score was 2-2 after full time, and then in extra time Geoff Hurst made the disputed third goal, then confirmed the win by scoring a last-minute goal to take the score to 4-2. BBC commentator Kenneth Wolstenholme made the famous saying, 'Some people are on the pitch. They think it's all over... It is now!'

*

Chas and I booked a week's holiday in a guesthouse in Bournemouth for our summer holiday in 1966. As we weren't married, Mum didn't want any 'hanky panky' and wouldn't allow us to go on our own, so I booked them in a guesthouse – but not the same one as ours. So, on a lovely Saturday in August, we all set off in Dad's Austin A40 down towards the south coast. It was glorious weather for the whole week and Dad even had to buy a straw hat to stop the sun from burning his head. Who needs to go abroad? But by then foreign holidays were not exclusively for the rich. Tour operators began offering cheap 'package holidays' from the 1950s, and by the 1960s the annual summer exodus to the Mediterranean with expectations of sun, sangria, and maybe sex, was the norm for many people. The south coast of Spain, the Costas, was the most popular destination.

Until the 1950s Benidorm had been a small town of sea-farers and fishermen known for their prowess at catching tuna, but tuna-fishing was in decline. The young Mayor of Benidorm, Pedro Zaragoza, set out a new future for his town, a vision of Benidorm with skyscrapers, gardens, pools and tourists, which became a reality. Zaragoza allowed immodest bikinis on the beach and forbade the townsfolk from insulting anyone who dared to wear one. Remember, this was conservative Catholic Spain.

Britain benefited from the package holiday too. Foreign hotels had showers and en-suite bathrooms and a strange plumbing accessory, the bidet. So, on their return, Brits wanted the same facilities in their homes, and not have to go to an outside toilet, as many terrace houses had. British hotels and guesthouses had to improve their facilities too.

*

A disaster happened on my twentieth birthday, Friday 21 October 1966: the Aberfan Disaster. There were seven enormous tips of waste coal above a small village in the valleys of South Wales and at 9.15 on that morning, after several days of heavy rain, one of the tips collapsed and slid onto homes and a school, killing 116 children and twenty-eight adults. The pupils of Pantglas Junior School had arrived just minutes earlier for the last day of school before the half-term holiday. Almost half the children on the school register died, along with five of their teachers.

The tips had been built over underground springs and the National Coal Board had ignored warnings that they were unstable. In 1965 a petition against the tip above the school from mothers of children at Pantglas School was presented by Headmistress Ann Jennings to Merthyr County Borough Council. Ms Jennings and many of the petitioners' children died in the disaster.

Donations poured into an appeal initiated by the Mayor of Merthyr Tydfil and soon reached almost £1,750,000.

Lord Robens, the chairman of the National Coal Board, was totally callous and insensitive and would not accept any blame, but the tribunal into the disaster unanimously blamed the National Coal Board for its ignorance, bungling ineptitude and failure in communications.

Despite government opposition, and advised by the NCB, public pressure led to a decision to remove the remaining tips. Lord Robens saw no obligation on the NCB to pay the cost of their removal. The government made a grant of £200,000 towards the cost, and the trustees of the disaster fund were unlawfully forced to contribute £150,000. In 1997 the Labour government of Tony Blair repaid the £150,000 to the disaster fund which it had been induced to pay by the Labour government of Harold Wilson. No allowance was made for inflation or interest that would have been earned.

The Mines and Quarries (Tips) Act of 1969 was designed to prevent disused tips constituting a danger to members of the public. Pantglas School was demolished and the Aberfan Memorial Garden now stands on the site. Green fields now grow where the tips used to be.

*

About this time Ken came to work in our office. He had moved to Australia with his family under the Assisted Passage Migration Scheme, created in 1945 after the Second World War, or '£10 Poms' as Australians called the British migrants. Over a million and a half Britons were seduced by government propaganda films in glorious technicolour, promoting the dream of a new life in the sun. Australia desperately wanted white British stock to live there and build its growing post-war economy. Assisted migrants had to remain in Australia for two years or refund the cost of their assisted passage and pay their own passage back to Britain. About 250,000 migrants decided to return home to Britain, but about half of those ended up going back to Australia, thus earning the name 'Boomerang Poms'.

Ken wanted to stay in Australia, but the rest of his family wanted to come back home, so they waited for the two years and then they all returned. I thought I might fancy going to live in Australia, but only had clerical skills and didn't have any training. Chas soon talked me out of it. I actually had a first aid certificate, and one of the lads we knew in the Civil Service went out to work as a medical orderly at Woomera Rocket Range apparently on the strength of his first aid certificate!

At least we had a choice, not like the children sent to Australia, New Zealand, Rhodesia and Canada from children's homes in Britain after the Second World War. It was a policy to save money, as the cost of keeping a child in an institution in Australia was about ten shillings, 10% of the cost of about £5 to keep a child in a British institution. Also it boosted the white stock in these Commonwealth countries. So children, some as young as four years old, were deported from well-respected charities including Barnardo's, the Salvation Army and the Catholic Church. None of this came to light until Margaret Humphreys, a social worker in Nottingham, received a letter from a woman in Australia saying that she had been shipped out to Australia at the age of four and wanted to trace her family. This would never have happened, or would it? On further investigation, Margaret Humphreys found out the astonishing truth that indeed it did happen.

Hampered by the authorities and often using her own money and resources she found that children were told their parents had died, and then they were offered a promise of a better life with 'oranges and sunshine' (the name of a feature film made in 2011) and so off they were shipped into the unknown. They were cast off from Britain with no birth records, no follow-up checks, and all connection with family, country and past was severed. British institutions effectively washed their hands of these poor children, who were often abused physically, mentally and sexually in Christian Brothers institutions such as Keaney College, Bindoon and Fairbridge Farm School in Australia. Far from being adopted by families in Britain, as their relatives were told, they were used as child labour and forced to work in horrific conditions. Unbelievably the 'Home Children' scheme was not terminated until the 1970s.

Margaret's investigations led to the establishment of the Child Migrants Trust in 1987, initially financed by her employer, Nottinghamshire County Council, to try and reunite the migrants with their parents and relatives. They were under great pressure, as time was running out, to find elderly relatives before they all died. Public apologies were made by the Australian Prime Minister Kevin Rudd in 2009, and by Britain's Prime Minister Gordon Brown in 2010. Margaret Humphreys received many awards including a CBE in 2011.

*

A friend of mine hired a room in the West Park Hotel for a party to celebrate her birthday and Chas and I were invited. My drink at the time was vodka and orange or vodka and lime as I was reliably informed that it didn't smell on your breath. I had to go home and face my mum afterwards. She thought we had children's party games with sandwiches and jelly. I did not enlighten her. Because so much alcohol was drunk we got the use of the room for free on other Saturday nights.

Most of us did not have a car but in January 1967 a law was introduced in the UK by Transport Minister Barbara Castle which led to the introduction in October of the breathalyser. This curbed car jaunts to country pubs, and the pubs in town were spruced up to encourage drinkers, so places like the West Park became more popular. Previous sobriety tests such as making drivers stand on one leg or walk in a straight line were upgraded to a more scientific approach to check if the blood alcohol level was above 80mg of alcohol per 100ml, the new legal limit. This legislation reduced deaths and serious injuries on the road.

A requirement for anchorage points for seatbelts in cars was introduced in 1965, followed by the requirement in 1968 to fit three-point belts in front seats of all new cars and all existing cars back to 1965. This also reduced road deaths, but the wearing of seatbelts did not become compulsory until 1983. Meanwhile, the Motorcycle (Wearing of Helmets) Regulations 1973 came into force and that also reduced serious injuries and road deaths. That regulation was amended by the Motorcycle Crash Helmets (Religious Exemption) Act 1973 allowing Sikhs to wear a turban instead of a crash helmet.

*

In March 1967 the Torrey Canyon oil tanker filled with 120,000 tons of crude oil went aground off Land's End. In an effort to reduce the size of the oil spill, the British government decided to set the wreck on fire by using Royal Air Force jets and Royal Navy planes to drop bombs and aviation fuel on the ship. High tides put the fire out, so bombing continued until the ship finally sank. The beaches on the south coast of England were contaminated and about 15,000 sea birds died, along with huge numbers of marine organisms. The beaches of France and Spain were also damaged by the 270-square-mile oil slick, and matters were exacerbated by the use of so-called detergents on the beaches, which were actually 'solvent emulsifiers'. Harold Wilson and his Labour government were strongly criticised for their handling of the incident.

The grounding of the supertanker caused an international and environmental legacy which led to many changes in legislation. At the time it was the world's worst oil spill, and remains the worst spill in UK history.

*

Colour television was launched by BBC2 on 1 July 1967 with live coverage from the Wimbledon Championships. It was a few years later before I watched Wimbledon in colour and I was amazed at how worn the courts were on the service line. In black and white the whole court looked a uniform grey. Our TV pictures now are so clear when I think back and realise what we watched in the early days of TV. TVs are so much sleeker and lighter with

Our wedding day. Christine is a bridesmaid, with Chas's niece Christine, another bridesmaid, and nephew Ian as pageboy.

flat screens, but that is to the detriment of the sound quality. Hopefully that will improve one day soon too.

*

We also went to dances on a Saturday night in the Civil Service Sports and Social Club at St George's Road 'huts' where we worked. Our friends Ann and Pete took us with them in their old car and we drank and jived at the popular venue. When the club upgraded their furniture, the chairs and Formica-topped tables were sold off. That is how Chas and I acquired our yellow-topped kitchen table and four chairs for £2 which we used in our first bungalow at 51 Meadowcroft.

As with the 'small stamp' there was another 'perk' available to women, which actually wasn't. That was the marriage gratuity given by some large companies to women to retain their employment before they got married. From the early 1960s to the 1980s women who worked for banks, insurance companies, British Telecom, the Post Office and Civil Service unwittingly gave up important pension rights in exchange for a paltry cash lump sum which was regarded at the time as a company perk. In the Civil Service the term was eight years' employment before marriage. It was rarely explained that by taking the marriage gratuity, women would wipe out thousands of pounds' worth of their future pension rights. As with the reduced National Insurance payments, this loss of pension rights was not realised until approaching retirement. Chas and I were going to wait to get this lucrative perk, as we thought, but in the end luckily decided not to. Our friends Ann and Pete waited for her marriage gratuity and put the money towards a new car.

On a cold morning at 11am on 21 October 1967, which happened to be my twenty-first birthday, my dad gave me away at St. Luke's Church and Chas and I were married. In Great Britain it is estimated 1544 people now share the surname Wardman, and it is the 7598th most common name. On that day I changed my surname to Dodsworth. We had our wedding reception in the Imperial Room above Bettys Café. In those days English weddings were usually on a Saturday and about lunchtime, so that the wedding reception was held in the afternoon, followed by the honeymoon. There was a rail strike at the time and Chas and I were not sure if our train would be running, but luckily it was. We arrived at Harrogate railway station and were waved off on the train to York, and there caught a train on to London. This train was full of newly-weds and was like a honeymoon express and the young couple sitting opposite us shared some of their wedding cake with us. Meanwhile most of the wedding group decided to continue celebrating at the Dragon Hotel at the top of Bilton Lane. After a few days in London, Chas and I went to Deal to spend a week with my Auntie Freda, Uncle Bill, John and young cousin Brian.

Changing Harrogate

Between the First and Second World Wars Harrogate began to decline as a spa town. In December 1926 Harrogate featured in the headlines of national newspapers. Agatha Christie, the celebrated author, was discovered staying at the Swan Hydro (now the Old Swan Hotel). She had been missing from home. Her disappearance triggered a huge search, including the first missing person inquiry in which aircraft were used. After ten days, Bob Tappin, a banjo player at the hotel, recognised her and alerted the police. The publicity was very good for Harrogate, but it was still in decline. The Victoria Baths were closed and the Municipal Orchestra was disbanded. The Pump Room, where visitors came to sample the waters, began to lose money and closed. Eventually, in 1953, it was turned into a museum telling the story of the spa.

The council decided that investment and improvements were needed to maintain Harrogate's eminence as a spa, so in 1924 new golf greens and tennis courts were opened in the Valley Gardens to encourage visitors and provide amenities for them. Toilets were added and lighting installed and an oval children's paddling pool was built. The Sun Pavilion and Sun Colonnade were opened in 1933 and the spring and autumn flower shows were held in the Valley Gardens the following year. In the 1950s I went with my mum on a Monday evening to the variety shows in the Sun Pavilion and on sunny Sundays in the summer our family walked down to the gardens from where we lived on Cheltenham Parade. We had ice creams and I would tuck my dress up and paddle in the children's pool along with other children who were paddling or sailing their boats.

Theatres and cinemas have opened and subsequently closed in Harrogate over the years but the Streamline Moderne Art Deco Odeon cinema which opened in 1936 on East Parade is still open. It was the first Harrogate cinema to be converted into mini-cinemas but still retained its original signage until recently. It was awarded Grade II listed building status in 1988 and featured on a 19p postage stamp in 1996. The original Odeons were the popular amphitheatres of Ancient Greece. Odeon cinemas in Britain were opened by Oscar Deutsch in the late 1920s and early 1930s. His publicity team claimed Odeon stood for 'Oscar Deutsch Entertains Our Nation'. I well remember queuing outside the Odeon and the Regal in the 1950s to see the popular British war films like *The Cruel Sea*, *The Dam Busters* and *Reach for the Sky* when cinemas still attracted large audiences.

One of the cinemas which closed was the Regal ABC, Associated British Cinemas Ltd. which opened in 1937 on Cambridge Road but closed in 1983 and was quickly demolished to be replaced by a parade of shops. It was this cinema where I usually went to 'Saturday morning pictures' with my friends in the 1950s.

The old market burnt down in 1937 and was replaced two years later. The beautiful tower that housed the great Potts clock which had been given to Harrogate by Charles Dickens' friend, Baroness Burdett-Coutts, survived the fire, but not the demolition of the market to make way for the Victoria Shopping Centre which was opened in November 1992 and houses the characterless high street chains. The shopping centre was built at the expense of the Victoria Gardens with the pond and fountain in the middle which are no longer there. Nor are the below-ground Victorian public toilets. The old market in my day was a lovely place filled with small local businesses, including the large greengrocer's stall owned by Christine's friend Angela Marsden's family. There were fish stalls, butchers, bakers, dairy, newsagent as well as kitchenware, shoes, clothes, curtain material and records. Downstairs was Robell's Music Box where we listened in booths to the 'B' side of records before we decided to buy them. The chap who ran the stall worked there for years. It had sheet music and row upon row of records arranged in a square around his seat. Years later I went back and he was still sitting there surrounded by his records. I also bought my first kitchen curtain material from the fabrics shop on the ground floor. I hand-stitched the bright red and yellow curtains because I did not have a sewing machine.

During the Second World War large numbers of civil servants were evacuated from blitz-torn London to Harrogate. Parliament, the Cabinet and top levels of the Civil Service, together with the administration, were even more concentrated in and around Whitehall in London than they are today. The destruction of Whitehall, including the deaths of the decision makers, civil servants, vital communications and transport, would completely disrupt government. So in 1936 the Warren-Fisher Committee proposed evacuating government staff from the Whitehall area to sites relatively safe from air attack. 'First line staff' required to run the war effort would initially move ten miles north of London, but if air attacks drove the government from London completely, this group would move into towns further away. The Admiralty, War Office and Air Ministry would be evacuated to towns including Harrogate.

The Post Office started to increase the telephone and telegraph capacity including installing many new lines. In the first few weeks of the war these moves were implemented, with some 8900 people moving to Harrogate and Bath. In Harrogate they were quartered at the big hotels which became office blocks. The workers became known as 'guinea pigs' because they paid a guinea a week in rent. During the war the single-storey terrapin huts off St George's Road were built as hospital accommodation in case there was a need. This was not necessary and they became used for Civil Service offices for the Post Office Savings Bank (where I started work in 1963); Ministry of Agriculture, Fisheries and Food; and the Air Ministry, part of the Ministry of Defence. Jim Carter, the well-known film and TV actor, most recently known for his role as Charles Carson, the butler in *Downton Abbey*, was born in Harrogate in 1948, so he is a couple of years younger than me. His father worked for the Air Ministry and his mother had been a land girl before working as a school secretary. Jim Carter went to Ashville College in Harrogate and was head boy in his final year.

There was also another government agency on Skipton Road in Harrogate: the Milk Marketing Board which controlled milk production and distribution in the United Kingdom. Their adverts on TV included slogans 'full of natural goodness' and 'drinka pinta milka day'. Those were the days when our milk was delivered daily by a milkman and the glass pint bottles were left on our doorstep. Now we collect our milk from the supermarket in Tetra Paks in different sizes, and in litres, skimmed, semi-skimmed and whole milk, and various other options.

Harrogate's bus station opened in 1938, near the central railway station, and the red West Yorkshire Road Car Company buses ran from there. The bus station clock was a feature in the town and 'Meet you under the bus station clock' was the usual arrangement for dating. There have been several alterations to the bus station since. The old railway station was largely demolished in 1965 and replaced by a towering concrete utilitarian station block which coincided with the loss of three main routes through the town because of the Beeching Axe. Britain had the first and greatest rail network in the world, shaping our Industrial Revolution, but the system had grown haphazardly and some closures and reorganisation were desperately needed. The then Conservative Prime Minister, Harold Macmillan, provided a brief to make the loss-making railways profitable. Ernest Marples, who was the Transport Minister and was associated with the successful high-profile road construction company Marples Ridgway, appointed Dr Richard Beeching from the board of ICI to be Chairman of the British Transport Commission in 1961. Beeching had no knowledge or experience of the railway industry but was paid the controversial annual salary of £24,000, the same as he had at ICI. The Prime Minister's annual salary was £10,000. Beeching's salary was thirty-five times the pay of many railway workers and has been described as a 'political disaster'.

Britain's railways were nationalised in 1948 and were losing large amounts of taxpayers' money. Beeching proposed closing 55% of stations and 30% of route miles, mostly rural and industrial lines. His decision was made purely on economic grounds with no thought to the social and cultural implications. So, about a hundred years after railways had brought prosperity to rural areas, these lines were mostly closed down, leaving the inhabitants without any public transport. Road traffic congestion was a serious problem, even when Beeching published his report, and the rail closures forced more people on to the already crowded road system. Some rail closures made very few savings but were a huge social loss and a destruction of our heritage. Beeching's second report in February 1965 setting out more rail closures was rejected by the government and he left the British Railways Board with a life peerage and returned to ICI. By 1968 the railways had not been restored to profitability and the plan to replace rail services with buses also failed.

Nowadays restored heritage lines and steam trains are hugely popular. They are run mostly by volunteers who refused to see a major part of our heritage slip away. By using their skills, hard work, patience and often financial backing they operate nearly 150 heritage and preservation lines.

The Northern Horticultural Society was founded in 1946 and opened the Harlow Carr Botanical Gardens in 1950 as a trial ground for assessing the suitability of plants for growing in northern climates. The Royal Horticultural Society merged with the Northern Horticultural Society in 2001 and acquired Harlow Carr Gardens. There is a Bettys Café Tea Rooms and shop there too. Geoffrey Smith was the Superintendent of the gardens from 1954 to 1974. When he left Harlow Carr and the tied cottage there, he bought Mount Pleasant Farm on the outskirts of Kettlesing near Harrogate, which was shown on his TV gardening programmes, and lived there until his death in 2009. He wrote gardening books and became a genial and knowledgeable radio and TV broadcaster including being presenter of *Gardeners' World* on TV from 1980 to 1982 and a panellist on *Gardeners' Question Time* from 1983 for twenty years. Some quotes of his – 'Put the brown end in the soil, the green end above it, and you're in with a much better chance', 'Plants need as much pampering as women', 'I don't feel as if I'm eating pound notes when I pick strawberries from my own plants' – demonstrate typical Yorkshire humour. There is a lovely commemorative stone to Geoffrey Smith near the stream at Harlow Carr with a verse from a poem by Dorothy Frances Gurney:

> *The kiss of the sun for pardon*
> *The song of the birds for mirth*
> *One is nearer God's heart in a garden*
> *Than anywhere else on earth.*

When flying down from Glasgow airport to Yeadon airport (Leeds/Bradford) one evening in 1983 Geoffrey Smith checked in at the Dan Air desk. I was working for Dan Air at the time, only for a year before we moved to Berkshire. I told him how much I enjoyed his TV programmes. He beamed at me and said, 'Do you really? That's very nice of you to say so.' He seemed a genuinely nice man. While I worked at the airport I either saw or checked in a few well-known people. I saw John Cleese, who looked as if his normal gait was like his 'Ministry of Funny Walks'! Bonnie Tyler, the singer, arrived on a Dan Air flight one evening wearing tight black leather trousers. The Flying Pickets flew down to Birmingham before performing on the BBC1 TV programme *Pebble Mill at One* at the now-defunct Pebble Mill Studios which closed in 2004. There were several sports teams at the airport who were flying off to appear at various venues. Cutting quite a dash as they arrived in matching outfits carrying large amounts of sporting equipment, they turned a few heads. The Harlem Globetrotters checked in one day and their heads were way over the pelmets above the desks. I also remember checking in a political contingent during the 1983 General Election (which gave the Conservative Party under Margaret Thatcher the most decisive election victory since the Labour Party in 1945 as we had won the Falklands War the previous year). Geoffrey Howe was there as well as Kate Adie, Joe Paley and cameramen of the BBC. The cameramen bought a seat for some of their precious expensive cameras to fly with them in the cabin. I especially remember Joe Paley as he was the last to check in for the flight and the conveyor belt stopped with his bag halfway through the curtain. When I came back to the desk after checking in the passengers for the flight (Dan Air did not have as many staff as companies such as British Airways and we had to double up on duties) I was mortified to find his luggage still there! I digress.

The Great Yorkshire Show acquired a permanent site off Wetherby Road in 1950. The showground had flower displays in marquees, craft and cooking. There were also cow byres for animals entering the show competitions and there was show jumping in the central arena. In 1957 the Great Yorkshire Show celebrated its centenary. The Queen and the Duke of Edinburgh visited the show that year and I recall us all having the day off primary school to line James Street and wave flags as their cavalcade passed by. The show is now the largest agricultural show in England and is still held over three days here in July each year. I visited the show in the 1960s with my friends from the grammar school and we enjoyed tasting the produce in the marquees and I remember seeing the famous Harvey Smith in the show jumping arena. Despite being descended from a long line of farmers, I did not enjoy the smell and muck in the cow byres and I am sure that I would never make a farmer!

Harrogate Borough Council set out to promote the fact that the town enjoyed a centrally geographical position in the country. It is about 200 miles south of Edinburgh and 200 miles north of London. It is also equidistant from the east and west coasts. The council pointed out that for postal and distribution reasons Harrogate was in an ideal situation and persuaded large firms to establish their administrative and scientific centres here. ICI Fibres Division was one of them. They experimented with clothing made from synthetic fibres. In the 1950s Crimplene was invented at the ICI laboratories in Harrogate, named after the nearby Crimple Beck. Someone I knew had a sister who worked at ICI and she was given clothes to wear and wash at home to see how they fared.

Another employer was the Tobacco Research Council. In the 1950s studies were published which suggested that smoking was associated with an increase in the incidence of lung cancer and bronchitis. In the UK tobacco companies responded by supporting research. In 1962 purpose-built research laboratories were constructed in Harrogate to develop reliable tests to measure the biological effects of tobacco smoke. The hypothesis was that tobacco smoke affects the respiratory system and produces changes which, in some smokers, could lead eventually to lung cancer. The aim was to identify the chemical compounds in tobacco smoke and modify the design of cigarettes to make them less harmful. The Harrogate laboratories used mouse skin-painting as its main test to assess the biological activity of tobacco smoke. The mice had their backs shaved and then a very high concentrate of tobacco smoke was applied. The scientists also developed a system for exposing laboratory animals to whole fresh smoke. Various other tests were used to investigate other kinds of biological changes brought about by smoke exposure, and to look at the efficacy of filters to prevent or reduce such changes. There was also research into nicotine and its effect on brain activity, blood pressure and behaviour and performance. The research into mouse skin-painting did not produce any definite results into which compound in cigarettes and smoke was responsible for lung cancers. The programme was wound down, having been taken as far as it profitably could. To this day there is no agreement among scientists as to which specific chemical compounds in tobacco smoke are responsible for the increased incidence of lung cancer and other diseases in smokers.

The Dunlopillo Division of the Dunlop Rubber Company was attracted to Harrogate. They produced latex foam mattresses, pillows, cinema seating and latex foam cushioning for cars. It was a large employer at its factory in the Pannal area of Harrogate but the company eventually transferred to Oldham in 2003. One of our first purchases for our new home when we got married in 1967 was a Dunlopillo mattress bought from the Co-op in the sale for £48 reduced from £60. We bought this with the extra money we earned working overtime in the winter. It was still a lot of money considering we were not well paid as young civil servants near the bottom of the pay scales. It would be more than a month's salary for one of us and equal to about £800 in today's money.

In 1952 Harrogate was twinned with Bagnères-de-Luchon, a spa and floral town in the French Pyrenees. Town twinning was the result of determined efforts to foster European co-operation and friendship after the horrors of the Second World War, and Harrogate's twinning with Luchon is reputedly the oldest in the country. The once-flourishing link, which included school exchange visits, faltered but there have recently been attempts to rejuvenate it. The award-winning Tewit Youth Band from Harrogate visited Luchon in August 2012. The St. John Fisher Tour de France cycling team completed a gruelling cycling event over four mountain passes in 2013. Harrogate hosted the Grand Départ of the Tour de France cycle race in 2014. Because of its geographical position Luchon is the fourth most visited town by the Tour de France.

Harrogate became a major exhibition and conference centre hosting many annual exhibitions and fairs. In 1959 the first purpose-built event halls were erected followed by further halls. This was at the expense of the beautiful Rose Gardens, tennis courts and children's playground where I used to play. There were two big stone lions on either side of the wide steps leading into the gardens, but it was all demolished. The stone lions were relocated to the Harlow Carr Gardens. In 1982 the huge International Centre was opened and hosted the 1982 Eurovision Song Contest which was watched by 800 million television viewers worldwide when it was broadcast by the BBC.

The British Tourist Authority set up the Britain in Bloom competition in 1963 in response to a similar project in France called Fleurissement de France, and Harrogate began to participate. The categories were widened in the 1970s to make competition fairer between larger cities, towns and villages, and Harrogate has won its category many times.

The first Harrogate International Festival took place in 1966 and has grown to include the Harrogate Music Festival, Theakston Old Peculier Crime Writing Festival, and the Literary Festival, History Festival and

Children's Festival. Events are held in venues around Harrogate including the Old Swan Hotel and the Royal Hall. A fiftieth celebratory event has recently been held in the Royal Hall. I remember walking down Parliament Street one summer in the late 1970s with my children and watching the youth bands marching in a parade through the town.

In 1988 there was a fire in the Victorian Lowther Arcade. The fire only destroyed a portion of the arcade, but in 1996 the arcade, the Ship Inn and a row of Georgian stone cottages were demolished to make way for a new huge Marks & Spencer store, which decimated the historic centre of the town.

Duttons for Buttons had a shop in Lowther Arcade in the 1950s but has since relocated to Oxford Street, Harrogate and has reputedly the largest stock of buttons in Great Britain and possibly in Europe, with more than 12,000 designs, each displayed with sample buttons on the outside of the boxes. The business also has shops in York, Ilkley, Keighley and Leeds, and supplies buttons to the theatre, TV and film industry. Madonna wore Duttons buttons on all the costumes she wore in the film *Evita*. Nicholas Cage also wore their vintage fastenings on the clothes he wore in *Captain Corelli's Mandolin*. *Pirates of the Caribbean* used their buttons, and all the soldiers' jackets in the eighteenth-century drama *Boswell's Defence* were ordered from Duttons.

West of Harrogate, just outside the Nidderdale Area of Outstanding Natural Beauty, is RAF Menwith Hill, owned by the Ministry of Defence and leased to the United States Army Security Agency in the late 1950s. A high frequency radio monitoring station was established to monitor communications from the Soviet Union during the Cold War. The huge highly visible white radomes, known to everyone in Harrogate as 'golf balls', are very sophisticated listening devices. The site contains an extensive satellite ground station and has been described as the largest monitoring station in the world. It provides communications and intelligence support services to the United Kingdom and the United States of America. In 1966 the National Security Agency took on responsibility for the site using some of the earliest sophisticated IBM computers. The site is commanded by an RAF officer supported by RAF staff, with the majority of services provided by the United States Air Force. In 2012 there were 400 British and 1800 NSA employees. Some information stated that the base was due to expand as it became increasingly vital to US intelligence, but then because of improved technology, a streamlining operation was decided upon in 2014 to cut some service and civilian jobs at the site although this would not affect the mission.

The Cold War was a state of tension after World War II between the Western Bloc (USA, NATO and its allies) and the Eastern Bloc (the Soviet Union). Both superpowers were heavily armed in preparation for an all-out nuclear war. The Cold War lasted from about 1947 until 1991. The Berlin Wall was built in 1961 to prevent East Germans from escaping to the west and causing a drain of workers. It divided Berlin and also split families who lived on both sides of the wall. Many people managed to escape but many paid with their lives. The wall was a symbol of the Cold War and its fall in 1989 marked the approaching end of the war.

In 1949 George Orwell published his book *Nineteen Eighty-Four* about government surveillance and tyranny epitomised by Big Brother, the Party leader. People started saying, 'Big Brother is watching you', a quote from the book. Menwith Hill monitoring station is a symbol of 'Big Brother is listening to you'. Regular protests have been held near the base and a number of peace camps were established here in the 1980s and 1990s, as at Greenham Common near where we now live.

When I was a teenager in Harrogate in the 1960s we used to see the Americans come into town for their nights out. The Harrogate lads resented the Americans if they fraternised with the local girls. It was a throwback to the Second World War when American GIs (so called because all their equipment was labelled 'Government Issue') that were stationed in Britain called the Brits, 'Underpaid, undersexed and under Eisenhower'. The Brits had responded describing the Americans as, 'Overpaid, oversexed and over here'. They were also regarded as overdecorated, overstaffed, overmaintenanced and overbearing!

The lads from the Army Apprentice College on the outskirts of Harrogate were noticeable with their short military-style haircuts, and were resented too.

Near Menwith Hill, just off the A59 near Blubberhouses (remember, it's a corruption of blaeberry or bilberry or maybe blowers) you can now find Thruscross Reservoir which was completed in 1966 to provide water for the growing population of Leeds. The village of West End was abandoned and a dam was constructed to create the reservoir. Trees were felled and the bodies from the graveyard were exhumed and buried on higher ground. The once-thriving flax mill, houses, farm cottages, school, bridge, church and graveyard were submerged. Now, when the water level drops during severe droughts, the church spire can be seen again. The Yorkshire-born author Peter Robinson bases his crime novels in Yorkshire as well as Canada where he lives now. The geography described in his novel *In a Dry Season* indicates that he based the location of Hobb's End on the village of West End.

By 1997 the Royal Hall was in need of restoration, and in 2000 English Heritage put the building on the national 'buildings at risk' register. The Royal Hall Restoration Trust was formed to restore the century-old venue to its former glory. Edward Fox, a grandson of Samson Fox, an original benefactor, supported the restoration. Donations were received from the council, Harrogate International Centre, the Heritage Lottery Fund and local benefactors. An authentic restoration and redecoration ensued and on 22 January 2008 Prince Charles, as the patron of the trust, attended the official reopening. Local artist Alister Colley recorded the reopening with paintings of the exterior of the building, and the interior on the opening night. The Royal Hall now boasts lapis lazuli on the inside of the dome, marble pillars, red plush seating and abundant glittering gold leaf paint. Some of the door handles are made in the shape of cockerels, which is a symbol of a spa town. Another spa symbol is a serpent, and the seats in the Valley Gardens are supported by wrought iron serpents.

The Majestic Hotel suffered another devastating fire in 2010 which claimed the life of an employee and resulted in severe water damage during the firefighting operation. The hotel was closed for four months, then partly reopened while other parts of the hotel were refurbished. The leisure club had a makeover, the murals in the lounges were restored and redecorating and carpeting completed. The Victorian property still has its Venetian chandeliers, grand public rooms and spa murals which run the full length of the Great Lounge.

Harrogate used to be in the West Riding of Yorkshire. From 1889 to 1974 Yorkshire was divided into three historic subdivisions called Ridings (North, East and West). Unlike most English counties, which were divided into hundreds, Yorkshire, due to its size, was divided into Thrydings (ancient Norse word for thirds). Harrogate was in the West Riding but with local government reorganisation on 1 April 1974 it lost its autonomy, its Mayor and its identity and became part of the over-large authority known as 'North Yorkshire'.

We moved away from Harrogate in 1971 and in 1980 St. Luke's Church, where we were married in 1967, was closed and turned into flats!

The government offices, 'the huts', on St George's Road where I worked for the first eight years of my working life were closed as the departments were relocated around the country. National Savings went to Glasgow. The Ministry of Defence was on the site, as well as the Ministry of Agriculture, Fisheries and Food and they were relocated too. The site was razed to the ground and was redeveloped as housing. Change indeed!

But many things remain great about Harrogate. The unique green necklace, the Stray, still surrounds it. It is a thriving shopping, conference and exhibition centre and has been voted as one of the best and happiest places to live in Britain. Long may it remain so.

Epilogue

After my mum was diagnosed with multiple sclerosis a few years after Geoffrey died, Dad and I helped a lot at home, but Mum was never satisfied. She was the kind of person whose 'cup is half empty' and for whom the 'grass is always greener on the other side'. I was married, as my parents had predicted, and left home. Chas and I bought our brand new two-bedroom bungalow at 51 Meadowcroft for £2,450.

Uncle Tom wanted to move to Freckleton, near Preston in Lancashire, after he retired. There was a mobile home park next to an RAF airfield and Tom planned to move there. So Mum and Dad bought a mobile home there when Dad retired at sixty-five so they would be near Tom. They went off for drives and days out, but as usual, Mum was not happy. Tom never did move there and died in 1976 when he was sixty-eight, so Mum and Dad moved back to Harrogate and bought a bungalow in Meadow Way, near Meadowcroft in Bilton. By then Chas and I lived in Scotland because Chas had been promoted to the National Savings office there. Dad had a major heart attack in December 1977 just after he got out of bed one morning. The doctor decided he should stay at home and not go into hospital, and he recovered to some extent, and carried on. A few months later, on 9 September 1978 he went to the Scarborough Hill Climb with a mate, Jack, who drove there. Walking back to the car afterwards, Dad collapsed and died. He was sixty-eight years old.

Mum always wanted company and she often said she 'needed constant care and attention' and wanted to go into a home, not like most people who want to avoid them. Anyway she sold their bungalow and managed to get a one-bedroom apartment in The Yorkshire home at the bottom of Cold Bath Road with a communal lounge and lovely views of Montpellier from her front window. There was a warden, and trips out were arranged and entertainment in the lounge. But, as usual, Mum was not satisfied. She did not have Dad to curb her moods and she got a taxi driver to move her and a few belongings into another home, one of a few she moved to. She avoided any help from me and played one person off against another. Eventually she ended up in the Royal Bath Hospital and died there on 10 October 1991, a few days after we had been to visit her from Berkshire, where we now live. We never really got on together, but she was still my mum.

*

I went to creative writing classes when I retired. One day our course tutor, Philip Scott, suggested we write about something traumatic which happened in our childhood; so I wrote the chapter 'Being Thirteen'. When I was young we did not ask our parents about their history or their memories, so I know very little about their early lives, and even less about my grandparents. During years of family history research I found out a lot and was able to piece some events together, so I thought I should write something about my family history. Chapters on my grandmas followed, and the story began. I found it much harder than making up stories, as I had in the creative writing classes, and put the writing aside for a long time. But when I revisited the writing and progressed, I realised I had to finish it and found the writing and research very interesting.

*

I have written this story primarily for my two daughters, two grandsons and three granddaughters. I suppose, in a way, it is a tribute to my ancestors too, as their sacrifices should never be forgotten. The story grew like Topsy, so I thought I would try and publish it. I did not include any boyfriends, except Chas, because there is not a lot to tell really, only a few short romances. I stopped at the date I was married, and my children can write their own stories, if they wish. This year, 2017, is our Golden Wedding.

Remember the past, live in the present, and look to the future.

Appendix

The Wardman Ancestors

1. Dyke Bottom Cottage still exists and still has a rare medieval 'cruck' wall, made with a timber frame, known as a wattle and daub construction. The daub is a rough lime-based plaster usually containing animal hair, dung and locally found aggregates.

2. In June 2013 my hubby and I walked the Link route from Harrogate to Ilkley to connect to the Dales Way long-distance walk. We walked from the Valley Gardens in Harrogate, past Haverah Park, Fewston and alongside Swinsty Reservoir and the village of Timble to Ilkley (birthplace of Alan Titchmarsh, gardener, TV presenter and novelist). We then walked the Dales Way to Bowness-on-Windermere. We took a week, walked nearly one hundred miles, used about 6400 calories and I took 220,000 steps! It was a wonderful walk taking in the Yorkshire Dales.

3. Some notes I took at Chatham on the history of the Corps of the Royal Engineers. There is a gap from 24 to 27 October.

1st November 1918.
Successful advance of Infantry. Sappers employed in working on road from our front line from east end of Sisto Ridge to Asiago.
   Advance of Division continued. Sappers work on road between Asiago and Campovere. Road cleared as far forward as Capitello. Orders received 11.00 for sappers to remain forward. Camp at Capitello

di Caltrano to be evacuated and all echelon to move forward to neighbourhood of Asiago.
During November.
Moved forward to east of Vezzena – Levico Caldonazzo – Bertoldi Road down into Caldonazzo was cut out of the sheer face of the cliff and very narrow and tortuous, and the horses and men considerably done up after trekking since 04.30 with only a 3 hour rest. It was decided to billet for the night at Lancin. 7 Austrian soldiers were found here and put under guard, and also a quantity of arms.

4th November.
Reached Caldonazzo by 09.15. Information received en route that an armistice was signed to take effect at 15.00 this day.

4. Extract from the *Harrogate Herald* on 23 January 1918:

In loving memory of Gunner Henry Wardman, RGA, nephew of the late Thomas Wardman, York Place, who died of wounds January 22nd 1917, after two years and five months continuous service.

'Into the field of battle
He bravely took his part
He fought and died for Britain
And the honour of his race'

5. The mitral valve is a valve in the left side of your heart between the two chambers, the atrium and the ventricle. Mitral valve stenosis, also known as mitral stenosis, is when the mitral valve opening in the heart is narrowed, usually because of rigidity or scarring, so that not enough blood can flow through it. Scarring caused by rheumatic fever is the leading cause of mitral valve stenosis. Rheumatic fever is usually a childhood disease and nowadays we have antibiotics to treat it. Apparently women are more at risk from mitral stenosis than men. I do not know if Cissie had rheumatic fever or scarlet fever, which is also a cause of the condition which might not occur until five or ten years after the fever.

Bibliography

Harrogate Grammar School Centenary by Malcolm Neesam

Exclusively Harrogate by Malcolm Neesam

Harrogate, Ripon, York & the Yorkshire Dales by Ward Lock & Co

History & Topography of Harrogate and the Forest of Knaresborough by William Grainge

Remembering Harrogate Cinemas & Theatres by Robert E. Preedy

Fewston Rediscovered by Claro Community

Harrogate Past by W. R. Mitchell

Bilton Historical Society publications

No Time to Wave Goodbye by Ben Wicks

How We Used to Live by Freda Kelsall

HMSO Civil Defence Handbook No. 10

The Great War: The Standard History of the World-Wide Conflict, Volume XII. Week ending 30 November 1918.

History of the Corps of Royal Engineers, Volume V, the Institute of Royal Engineers, 1952

Publications covering the Tirah Campaign by authors G. and J. Powell, and Major M. L. Ferrar